ALL YOU NEEDED WAS LOVE

Books by John Blake

ALL YOU NEEDED WAS LOVE:
The Beatles After the Beatles

UP AND DOWN WITH THE ROLLING STONES
(written with Tony Sanchez)

ALL YOU NEEDED WAS LOVE

The Beatles After the Beatles

JOHN BLAKE

A Perigee Book

Perigee Books
are published by
G. P. Putnam's Sons
200 Madison Avenue
New York, N.Y. 10016

Library of Congress Cataloging in Publication Data

Blake, John, date.
All you needed was love.

1. Beatles. 2. Harrison, George, 1943–
3. Lennon, John, 1940–1980. 4. McCartney, Paul.
5. Starr, Ringo. 6. Rock musicians—England—Biography.
I. Title.
ML421.B4B6   784.5'4'00922 [B]   81-5946
ISBN 0-399-50556-3   AACR2

First Perigee Printing, 1981
Designed by Bernard Schleifer

PRINTED IN THE UNITED STATES OF AMERICA

For Diane

ACKNOWLEDGMENTS

With thanks to all the lovely people who gave so freely of their time and without whom this book would not have been possible. But especially to Paul, Linda, and Ringo, to Denny Laine, Mike McGear, Harry Harrison, Bob Mercer, Tony Bramwell, Jackie Stewart, Tony Brainsby, Bill Harry, Eric Idle, and Robin Cruikshank. To Louis Kirby, Editor of the *London Evening Standard*, for generously allowing me both time to write this book and the opportunity to meet so many people who gave me assistance. To Robin McGibbon, Ellis Amburn and Roger Scholl for making it happen. To Rosie Ries and Mandy Bruce for their help with research and to Emma and Charlotte for the endless coffee.

CONTENTS

"There is no armor against fate;
Death lays his icy hands on kings."
—JAMES SHIRLEY

COME TOGETHER—
FALL APART

1

The Beatles broke up violently as a group and violence was to hound them as they pursued their separate paths in the decade to follow.

ON A PARTICULARLY cold day in February, 1970, a long, sleek Mercedes limousine whispered along Cavendish Avenue to halt majestically outside Paul McCartney's high, wooden front gate.

A gaggle of Paul's most loyal fans stood sentinel outside his big, psychedelically painted house in St. John's Wood. The girls had been hanging around there for years, chatting with Paul's visitors or with Rose, his bright, Cockney house-keeper. The girls' frustration on this day at their inability to view the occupant of the lavish limousine through the occult blackness of the windows was relieved when the chauffeur opened the rear door, and Ringo Starr stepped out.

"Ooh," whispered one of the girls. "Isn't he lovely?" Curiously, Ringo, who had always been unkindly labeled the ugly member of the Beatles, had become, with his luminously blue eyes and long, shining hair, considerably more attractive than his three colleagues, who all peered with worried eyes from behind the wild, unkempt beards of tired old men.

Today, however, Ringo seemed taciturn. He hastily signed the proffered autograph books, pressed the bell set into the wall, and spoke briefly into the intercom. Then, at the sound of a buzzer, he pushed the high front gate open to let himself into the courtyard. He walked past the Aston-Martin and the Mini, across the flagstones, up a few steps, and through the half-open front door.

"Hi," said Paul. "Good to see you. . . ." But Paul's eyes were wary, watchful. He had a pretty good idea why Ringo had come.

Ringo was acting in the role of messenger boy. John and George had both written letters which they wanted Paul to read. Slowly, in icy silence, Paul slit open the envelopes to glower at the enclosed notes.

"Look, Paul," said Ringo awkwardly. "You've got to understand. We can't put out your solo album yet. It isn't ready. We've got to put the *Let It Be* album out at the beginning of May."

Paul's face began to flush as he clutched his fists in an effort to control his rising temper; he knew that the only reason they didn't want his solo album released was because they were all afraid that it would do better than the dreadful *Let It Be* album. After all the months of work he had put into his independent debut, they were all ganging together to wreck everything for him.

"This is the last straw," he yelled at Ringo. "If you drag me down, I'll drag you down. . . ."

"He went completely out of control," Ringo said later, "prodding his fingers toward my face, shouting: 'I'll finish you all now,' and 'You'll pay.' He told me to put my coat on and get out. . . . While I thought Paul had behaved a bit like a spoiled child, I could see the release date of his record had a gigantic emotional significance for him. Whether he was right or wrong to be so emotional, I felt that since he was our friend and since the date was of such immense significance to him, we should let him have his own way. . . ."

Not long after Ringo's meeting with Paul in St. John's,

John Lennon was interrupted at home by a phone call. Mostly, John didn't bother to answer the phone when it rang at Tittenhurst Park. But, on this day, Thursday, April 9, 1970, the ringing was so persistent that he eventually turned down the sound on the television flickering at the end of his bed and picked up the receiver.

"Hello, John," said Paul McCartney. What the hell did Paul want, John wondered. Lately, communication between the two had been infrequent at best. "Look, I'm just ringing because I think you should be the first to know. I'm doing the same as you. I'm leaving the Beatles."

"Yeah," said John. "Yeah, great . . . at least two of us are thinking alike."

He put the phone down, went back to the television, and tried to concentrate. Suddenly, he felt very alone, very lost. He had wanted it to end for so long, and yet it was hard to envision life without the Beatles. . . .

A year and a half before, the movie *Get Back* had seemed to Paul the one idea which could save both the Beatles and Apple Corps, Ltd. He wanted it to become a totally integrated project, one which would use all the facilities Apple had at its disposal. He planned, in addition to the film, a book about the *Get Back* project from Apple's publishing division and a soundtrack LP from Apple's record division. He truly believed that all the Beatles had to do was to work together again and all their wounds would be healed.

The filming for *Get Back* had first started at International Recording Studios in Twickenham at 10 A.M. on January 2. From the moment John and Yoko shuffled in—late, bleary-eyed, and with their arms wrapped tight around one another like Abelard and Heloise—it was obvious that the project was not going to be easy. None of them besides Paul could really be bothered with all the hassle. Besides, the studio was a vast barn of a place chosen for the benefit of the film crew rather than for the Beatles, who were supposed to be shown recording their new album. It was bitterly cold and they were all miserable.

After all the trouble he had taken to set the project up, Paul was horrified to find the other three looking at him as though he was a particularly truculent schoolteacher and they were his reluctant and unfortunate pupils.

He tried to persuade them to rehearse because they had not played together for so long, but they only swore and moaned at him. In retaliation, Paul seemed to decide that he would be as bloody-minded as they appeared to think he was. When, for example, John started to play the first chords of a new song he had written, called "Across the Universe," Paul simply yawned and started to play boogie instead.

As the cameras rolled, Paul began nagging at George, needling him about the way he was playing guitar. George had just returned from the States where he had been jamming with numerous friends and, after all the adulation he had enjoyed there, he was furious at the way Paul was talking down to him. "Paul has shown a superior attitude toward me, musically, for years," he said. "In normal circumstances, I had not let this attitude bother me and, to get a peaceful life, I had always let him have his own way, even when this meant that songs which I had composed were not being recorded. When I came back from the States, I was in a very happy frame of mind, but I quickly discovered that I was up against the same old Paul."

George stomped off the set in a blue funk, telling Paul that he could find a new guitarist. But he returned on the following day after Paul apologized profusely to him.

In an attempt to salvage the project, they had decided to complete the filming and recording in the more comfortable surroundings of Apple's basement studio.

There was a small problem, however. Magic Alex, the electronics wizard who had fascinated the Beatles over the years with such inventions as paint that glowed when connected to electric currents and radios that could transmit music from a turntable in another room, had been commissioned to build a revolutionary seventy-two-track studio at Apple. No machinery, however, had been installed. In desperation, Paul had phoned the paternal, ever-patient George Martin, their producer, and Martin had agreed to move mobile equipment into the studio for the project. Despite the room's proximity to a thundering central heating boiler, the sound of secretaries stomping overhead, and the fact that Magic Alex had forgotten to include a hole for cables between the studio and the control booth, Martin somehow managed to save the day.

An icy wind blasted down Savile Row, slashing through the thin, clutched coats of scampering secretaries and shop assistants like a fish-gutter's knife. Sometimes it seems that there is nowhere more wretched on earth than London on a bleak January day. Even the Apple "scruffs," as the fans were labeled, had been driven to take refuge from the chill in the doorways of neighboring shops and offices. Yet today, January 30, 1969, there will be a little ray of sunshine amidst the gloom: After all the squabbling and the backbiting, the Beatles have decided to play together for the first time in nearly four years.

Paul had wanted them to play the Albert Hall or the Round House as the climax to *Get Back.*

"Only I'm not playing any fucking concert halls," John had said. And George had agreed with him.

So, diplomatically, Paul had agreed that they should play together anywhere the others liked—which turned out to be the roof of the Apple building on Savile Row.

While the film's director, Michael Lindsay-Hogg, and his assistants worked frantically to set up all the equipment before the feeble light finally died, the four Beatles sat in an office sipping tea, laughing, and joking. It was almost like the old days, hanging around in the dressing room, waiting to go on. Curiously, they all felt nervous: it had been so very long. They didn't look at all as they had the last time they had

played in concert together back in 1966; then they had all
worn the same long, shiny hairstyles and identically immaculate suits.

Now Paul, who seemed jangled and hurt by the festering
dislike the other three seemed to hold for him, wore a huge,
bushy beard, his hair combed severely back. John, clean-
shaven, draped his hair in a center-parted cloud—like Yoko's.
He peered at the world now through round, unflattering,
National Health-style spectacles. George, looking more gaunt
than ever, wore a Zapata mustache and an Apache hairstyle,
while Ringo just wore long sideburns and a mustache. Of all
of them, he was the only one who didn't look ravaged and
drawn.

"OK," said the ever-dependable Big Mal Evans, the Beatles' road manager. "Time to go." It was just like the old days.
Once George had picked out the opening chords, they
pumped exuberantly into their instruments. It felt wonderful
for them to be out of the studio, away from all the bickering,
simply doing what they were best at once again—making
music. They all felt it and grinned triumphantly at one
another as John bopped slowly up and down in his familiar
legs-wide-apart stance. None of them felt the Siberian wind
that cruelly whipped their hair around their faces. They were
high with the joy of being the Beatles once again.

Far below on the street, excited crowds blocked Savile Row
while office managers in pin-striped suits complained to the
police that the music was making it impossible for them to
concentrate on their work. Shortly afterwards, a squad of
pale, ugly policemen reached the Apple roof to tell the Beatles
to stop. But by then it didn't matter: they had recorded more
than enough songs for the film. Although they didn't know it
then, they had given the last performance they would ever
play as the Beatles.

If only the rest of the filming had been as magical as that
afternoon, they just might have stayed together.

But the resentment and ways in which they had grown
apart were proving too great to bridge. It was earlier that

month that John and Yoko Ono had first started using heroin. Many of their friends were on smack then—Robert Fraser, Keith Richards, Eric Clapton, Marianne Faithful—and, as a result, there was no problem in obtaining the stuff. They had tried it first at a friend's flat after they had been seething with rage and misery at the way in which the world had turned on them; the almost unbelievable fashion in which Fleet Street had slandered Yoko, describing her as "ugly," and "middle-aged," and "ruthless," as though writing of a criminal or someone who had no feelings or sensitivity whatever.

"And Paul and George are the worst of the fucking lot," railed John. "They're always making their cheap, snide little remarks about Yoko; always trying to do every little thing they can to fuck-up our love. Paul's even written a song about her. It's called 'Get Back,' and every time he sang the chorus in the studio I saw the way he looked at Yoko, like he was singing it to her. And I still can't believe the things George said to her, like he'd heard from New York that she'd got a bad vibe. I should have smacked him in the mouth but I still thought they would all come to love her once they knew her like I knew her."

John thought the employees at Apple hated her too, and he was determined to destroy anyone who failed to treat Yoko wtih all the love and respect she deserved.

"Yeah, sure, I know John thinks we *hate* her," Richard DiLello, Apple's house hippie and author of the hilarious book *The Longest Cocktail Party,* said at this time. "*Hate!* That's a very strong accusation and an extreme assumption. I can't say as I blame him for thinking that sometimes, but the reason he feels that way is because we don't *love* her. That's the truth. I'd be a liar if I said we love her, but we certainly don't hate her. If anything, we've just always wanted to get to know her better. It would be a welcome relief to walk into a room just *once* empty-handed, without an amplifier, without a cup of tea or a press cutting, without a list of people who want to interview them. . . . But we're all so insecure and afraid of our status in their eyes that we need all those fucking props! It's a bad gig being a rich man's slave. We can't get to know *her* or *them* any better because we've passively accepted the roles that have been assigned us and mindlessly act them out. . . .

"She's achieved Beatle status around here and there's nothing more intimidating than that. I know it's not her choice, but it's the reality just the same. When you hear the girls saying, 'Oh, I can't stand her; she's so difficult to please, so impossible to get on with . . .' you know where that's at! It's the slave's backlash, it's chicks being catty, it's their safety valve for letting off steam, but there's no real malice behind the words, there's no real substance to any of it. . . ."

John was angry and disillusioned. Smack, John's friend had told him and Yoko, would rejuvenate them, would make the pain go away. Listlessly, they had watched as he poured two lines of white powder onto a face mirror then chopped it into an even finer powder with the aid of a razor blade. He had calmly rolled a pound note into a thin tube and had invited them to use this improvised straw to sniff the powder into their noses. "You know that feeling when you get butterflies in your insides," John had told a friend later. "Well, this was like having a pair of golden eagles in your stomach."

They had both been violently sick after their first experience but they continued to snort heroin on a couple of subsequent occasions.

All through the filming and recording of *Get Back,* the Beatles had seemed to be searching desperately for their lost innocence. They had played everything that came into their heads, from the numbers they used to sing in Liverpool before they thought about recording, through a string of rock 'n' roll classics, on to their forlorn new songs like "The Long and Winding Road" and "Let It Be." When all the filming and recording was over, they were left with twenty-nine hours of taped music.

"The whole thing had been such an ordeal, like a fucking war, that not one of us could face even looking at the tapes— far less making them into an album," said John. And so the music sat in cans, ignored and gathering dust while the Beatles dealt with more pressing problems.

2

By 1965, THE SUCCESS the Beatles had fought and schemed and speeded for had already turned into an anaconda, slowly squeezing all normality and privacy from their lives. They turned to a newly popular drug, marijuana, to help them escape. Inevitably, it was John who was first to turn on. Bob Dylan offered him a joint when he visited John's mock-Tudor mansion in Weybridge during a concert tour of Britain. Pretty soon the four Beatles were smoking dope a great deal, giggling together in a world where no one could reach them from the moment they woke up. Cannabis became a door they could close against people whenever it all became too much. Ironically, the more the world envied, loved, and admired them, the more intolerable life was to become.

When the Beatles released "Help!" as a single in July, 1965, few people realized that it was a desperate *cri de coeur,* a heartfelt scream for some way out of the confusion.

It was, John was to say later, the song which best summed up his reaction to being acclaimed a demigod.

It had all gone from being wonderful to being insane so very quickly. On June 12, 1965, it was announced that the Beatles were to be made Members of the Order of the British Empire. To the middle-aged, staid middle class, the Beatles were dangerous radicals, underminers of all that was best in Britain.

"I can't believe it," John said. "I thought you had to drive tanks and win wars to get the M.B.E."

Nevertheless, receiving the M.B.E. medals was fun, which is more than could be said for the tours. There was no precedent for the Beatles, so Brian Epstein, their manager, had no example to guide him when it came to deciding just how many tours the Beatles could cope with. All he knew was that there were millions upon millions of dollars to be made by keeping the band working flat out, and if he stopped perhaps the money would dry up forever.

At every place they visited, there were new girls eager to bed a Beatle. And sex became almost an obsession for them, something real, warmth, being close to another human being in a world of fantasy, screaming children, and sycophants. "It was like us going through Fellini's *Satyricon*," John was later to recall. Amazingly, most fans knew nothing of the promiscuity of their idols, nor would they have believed it if they had been told. The Beatles, after all, weren't like that.

George and John began to spend a good deal of their time hallucinating as well. Their first acid trip turned out to be a trip from which neither of them ever completely returned.

Shortly before George and Patti Boyd's marriage in January of 1966, John and Cynthia, and George and Patti had gone to dinner with a dentist friend, whose main link with them— apart from their teeth—was a penchant for mind-addling chemicals. At that time, it was extremely easy for dentists to misappropriate a little cocaine from their offices. The gentleman concerned had won the everlasting admiration of John and George by introducing them to the glittering, white crystals.

When the four of them arrived for dinner, the crisp, white tablecloth was set with sparkling crystal and gleaming silver. They drank the finest wines, talked a little of philosophy and music, and touched briefly on the growing craze for LSD.

All through the meal, the dentist's girlfriend looked at them strangely, making them feel restless. They got ready to

George and Patti Harrison

leave as soon as they had finished their coffee. "No, you have to stay," the dentist said, gazing knowingly into Patti's eyes. "It's all about to happen."

"Blow this," whispered George. "We're in for an orgy."

But the dentist told him he had put LSD in their coffee. They didn't believe him—they felt perfectly normal. If they had taken speed or smoked some dope, they would have begun to feel the effects by now; anyway they were in the mood for excitement, they wanted to go out.

So the four of them set off for the Ad Lib Club in George's black-windowed Mini. The Ad Lib was the coolest, most exclusive club in the world. It was there the Beatles held court while the rest of rock clustered around begging for an audience like humble courtiers.

As they neared the club, John noticed that the streetlights seemed to burst at him like exploding flashguns as they passed by—but only when he saw them from the corners of his eyes. If he glowered at them, they seemed perfectly normal. A car hooted somewhere far away. He looked at George and realized they had stopped at a green traffic light. George was looking at the light as if mesmerized; when John urged him on, he only giggled. They felt as if they'd spent hours smoking grass—euphoric, stoned, and confused.

As they approached the Ad Lib, it seemed as if it was on fire; they could see blinding, flickering light shimmering from the building, and they laughed. "It's not on fire," said John after a few minutes. "It's just all lit up because they've got some big premiere party or something on there. Hey, let's go and dance outside. This is fantastic."

Cynthia began to cry.

"Hey," one of them screamed when they had somehow stumbled onto the pavement, oblivious to the curious stares of passersby, "let's smash a window."

They all collapsed on the pavement, their heads spinning Ferris wheels, the world a wonderful, Technicolor blur. John laughed until his insides began to ache.

Somehow they managed to fall into the club's elevator,

John Lennon, 1966

George, Cynthia, John and Patti traveling together

tittering like schoolgirls at a smutty movie. Suddenly, John pointed at a red light in the lift and screamed: "Fire!" Instantly, the giggling turned to terror as they tried to beat out the flames before they were destroyed. They were all terrified, terrified they would be burned to death. But the elevator doors opened and they stumbled into the club. They sat down, subdued and frightened now. John focused on the table in an effort to remember where he was, to escape the nightmare, but the table started to move and grow larger before his eyes. "I suddenly realized it was only a table," he explained, "with the four of us round it but it went this long, just like I had read—describing the effects of opium in the old days, and I thought: 'Fuck! It's happening.'"

People tried to speak to them but they could only gaze at glasses or the grain of the wood or at the carpet, listening to tiny sounds that suddenly seemed almost deafening.

Only by luck did they manage to find their way out of the club again, amazed at what was happening to them. As they climbed into the car, they suddenly burst out laughing. "Don't make me laugh," George pleaded—a plea he continued to repeat as the Mini slowly shuddered its way toward his home.

"George's house seemed to be just like a big submarine," said John. "I was driving it, they all went to bed. I was carrying on in it, it seemed to float above his wall, which was eighteen foot, and I was driving it."

John spent the rest of the night drawing strange, wonderful pictures which he later gave to Ringo. The experience profoundly moved John and George: they saw it, as Timothy Leary had, as a revelation, the opening of the door to their psyches.

Cynthia didn't see it that way at all: "It made me finally realize I was on my own," she said in her book *A Twist of Lennon*. "It was a horrifying experience that I will never forget, an *Alice in Wonderland* experience. I felt as though the bottom was beginning to fall out of my world. I never felt closer to insanity than I did then. . . ."

Life was never to be the same again for any of them.

Money, too, by this time ceased to have any meaning for the Beatles. One concert, at Shea Stadium in New York in 1965, grossed $304,000—a world record which stood for many years. Millions upon millions of dollars were crashing down on them like water from Niagara. "But it didn't make life wonderful for us," said Paul. "We were either working or locked up the whole time. There was no way we could go around spending it."

After John gave an interview to Maureen Cleave in the London *Evening Standard* in which he said the Beatles were more popular than Christ, the Ku Klux Klan swore enmity, and Beatle books, effigies, and records were turned into huge bonfires right across the Southern states. "Yeah, well, that was a drag," said John. "As if touring wasn't bad enough anyway, we had to put up with all that shit as well. We couldn't even hear ourselves sing when we went out on stage. The whole thing was becoming ridiculous."

The last concert ever given by the Beatles was at Candlestick Park in San Francisco on August 29, 1966. "We'd heard all the screaming and it was very, very loud," said Ringo. "We just didn't want to hear it anymore."

Symbolically, Brian Epstein missed the show. His briefcase—filled with illicit drugs, incriminating love letters, and photographs—had been stolen from his hotel room by a blackmailer. As the Beatles battered their exhausted way through their songs, he was desperately negotiating for its return.

They all flew back to London the next day, sighing with relief that they had fulfilled all the contracts, done everything they had agreed to do.

Even Paul seemed pleased, though he was bothered by a nagging feeling of loss. Of all the Beatles, he was the only one who liked the adulation, who needed constant reassurance that people adored him, which was odd really because he was the handsomest, and possibly the best musician, of them all.

George, curiously, was the only one who had the slightest idea of what he intended to do with his life after the Beatles' last tour—curiously, because George had always seemed no more than a craftsmanlike apprentice plodding doggedly in the phosphorescent footsteps of John and Paul. But George wasn't less intelligent than the others, merely younger.

John, Paul, and Ringo floundered like grounded whales desperately searching for something to occupy their days, now that the touring they had so loathed was over. George and his wife Patti, however, packed their expensive suitcases, took a chauffeur-driven limousine to Heathrow and boarded a plane for Delhi and the meaning of life.

That isn't actually what they told their friends, of course. They said they were going to India so George could study the sitar with the renowned Indian classical musician Ravi Shankar—George had taught himself the rudiments of playing sitar while fooling around, killing time on the set of the film *Help!* the previous year. But everyone close to the pair knew that LSD had left them with a feeling of spiritual vacuum, a craving to understand. They had become avid readers, first of Aldous Huxley, then of increasingly mystical, Oriental works. Both had been profoundly moved and affected by the book *Autobiography of a Yogi*.

Deep inside, though, George was a little wary of India; he had heard the horror stories of dead babies in dustbins, of plague and pestilence. But from the moment he walked out of the stinking, ramshackle airport building into the balmy sunshine of a land where everyone smiled, where people wanted to give and know, not grab and wound, he was in love, in the way that a man falls hopelessly in love with a beautiful, intelligent woman—forever unpeeling new delights, discovering new spiritual and emotional depths. It was a love affair that seemed destined to last all his life. When

George and Patti returned to England to celebrate Christmas at the end of 1966, their friends said they appeared to have developed a new contentment, an inner peace, as though they knew something nobody else could understand.

John, during this time, had been invited by his friend, Dick Lester, the producer, to star in a film called *How I Won the War*, being filmed in Spain. Once on the set, however, he found acting too contrived, actors too affected, and movies too slow after the fast, gritty, instant buzz of playing rock 'n' roll. Rapidly, he became bored, realizing that he lacked any real gift for acting.

But John's stay in Spain did have two fruitful consequences: while there he wrote "Strawberry Fields Forever," perhaps his most haunting song; he also began to think more and more of life as an individual, without the others.

"It did me so much good to get away for six weeks," he said. "It gave me time to think on my own, away from the others. From then on, I was looking for somewhere to go, but I didn't have the nerve to really step out on the boat by myself and push it off. . . ."

Paul, meanwhile, was almost ready to follow John, Ringo, and George into marriage. He had met Jane Asher, a London actress, three years previously when she had gone to see several pop groups—including the Beatles—so she could write a piece about them for *Radio Times*. Jane had all the poise and intellectual awareness that Paul craved. He was acutely aware that, despite everything, he was still essentially a provincial lad, and he longed to understand art and literature and music the way Jane did.

The four Beatles, in their search for happiness, had begun to splinter slightly apart into their individual components.

The Beatles were not alone among their rock contemporaries in feeling just a little lost: the fame and money had happened so very, very quickly—at the age of twenty-five so

John Lennon dressed for the BBC show "Not Only—But Also" in December of 1966

many of them had achieved all the things most people spend their whole lives striving for. Their friends—in the Moody Blues, 'the Who—all frenzied young men whose dreams had come true too soon, now sat in their grand, lonely homes wondering, like factory workers who have just won the state lottery, why there was still something missing from their lives.

One such close friend was Brian Jones, lead guitarist with the Rolling Stones. Brian was the most musically talented member of the band, and the one all the girls screamed over. Yet Brian seemed to have become more deeply enmeshed in drugs than any of them. He would go straight from one LSD trip to the next, as well as snorting handfuls of cocaine or mixing deadly cocktails of sleeping tablets and vodka. "They're destroying me," Brian rasped to John one night, after gulping down yet another huge slug of whiskey and coke. "I started the fucking band and now they keep trying to squeeze me out. It's all Jagger-Richards this, Jagger-Richards that. They won't even listen to my songs any more."

John and Brian had much in common: a kiss of genius, a dangerous charisma, and a yearning emptiness inside.

"You're just being paranoid, man," said John, though he knew Brian's fears were well-grounded in fact. "Look, I get sick of Paul sometimes, of the way he's forever trying to dominate me, but you have to stand up to these egomaniacs, you can't just get smashed out of your box. Look, how about if I ask you to play sax or something on some Beatle records, that'll make 'em all sit up and take notice, won't it?"

True to his word, John did invite Brian to play saxophone on two subsequent Beatles' records, but by then the wraiths were gathering. Brian Jones was already doomed.

John, Paul, George, and Ringo greeted one another like old lovers, however, when the time finally came in February of 1967 to start work on the new album. It was Paul who thought of the name for the record, *Sgt. Pepper's Lonely Hearts Club Band*. He was just playing around with odd words and phrases, the way he wrote most of his songs, when the title somehow seemed to come together. "They're a bit of a brass band in a way," said Paul. "But they're also a rock band because they've got the San Francisco thing."

But, though Paul dreamed up the title of the LP, the record was in every way a team effort. The cleverest track, "A Day in the Life," became a kind of memorial to John and Paul's songwriting partnership. John started writing the song with a copy of the *Daily Mail* propped up in front of him on the piano. He read a filler paragraph about four thousand holes being discovered in Blackburn, Lancashire, so he wrote that down; then Paul chipped in a couple of lines and gradually they created a mysterious, almost profound song between them, in the same way they had in the very early days. It was to be just about the last time the two of them were ever to collaborate fully and wholeheartedly on a number—though neither of them knew it at the time.

Although they were very close, Paul sensed intuitively that he was losing John: the one person he loved more than anyone in the world was subconsciously pulling away, seeking something that Paul was incapable of giving him. John's wife, Cynthia, also felt a premonitory shiver.

They were all talking and reading about religion and philosophy at this time, partly because acid had opened their minds to previously undreamed-of possibilities and partly because they desperately needed something to make sense of all the insanity surrounding them.

Patti, George's wife, was the first to join the Maharishi's Spiritual Regeneration Movement and the first to learn to meditate: the Beatles themselves were interested, but they were so busy recording *Sgt. Pepper* that there really wasn't time to become involved.

The Beatles first encountered the Maharishi at a lecture at the Park Lane Hilton on a Thursday in August. A great, rich gurgle seemed to bubble up from somewhere deep in his soul. He gave them flowers, talked a little of *karma,* and invited them all to join him the following Saturday for a weekend conference he was holding in North Wales.

The Beatles wanted Brian Epstein to come with them—they were worried about the quantities of drugs he was taking. But Brian was planning a small party the coming August Bank Holiday weekend at his mansion.

The scene at Euston Station on the Saturday morning of the conference was like a dervish battle. Thousands of fans crammed the concourse; there were enough reporters, photographers, and film crews to give excellent coverage to a small war and sufficient policemen to control a Cup Final crowd.

"This is farcical," Mick Jagger protested to Marianne Faithful when the pair of them arrived, hand-in-hand, at the train station to join the Beatles, the Maharishi, and others. "It's more like a circus than the beginning of a religious experience."

The press felt similarly: one newspaper headlined it "THE BEATLES' MAGICAL, MYSTICAL TRAIN."

At last all the Beatles and their friends seemed to be aboard, and the train pulled slowly out of the station. Suddenly, John's wail echoed through the carriage: "Oh, Jesus—we've left Cyn on the platform."

Poor Cynthia; though she had arrived early, a policeman had mistaken her for a fan and had refused to let her through the crowd. She stood, alone and sobbing, on the platform.

"What nobody could possibly understand," she said later, "was that my tears were not because I had missed the stupid train, but they were expressing my heartfelt sadness. I knew when I missed that train it was synonymous with all my premonitions for the future. I just knew in my heart, as I watched all the people that I loved fading into the hazy distance, that that was to be my future. The loneliness I felt on that station platform would become a permanent loneliness before very long, and I shivered at the thought."

To the Beatles, the Maharishi seemed like a miraculous catalyst which had the power to at last give their lives coherence. He told them most Westerners failed to come to terms with Eastern religions because so many gurus insisted that poverty was a prerequisite to spiritual enlightenment. In reality, said the Maharishi, it was the way in which a person behaved, not giving away possessions, which would help him to achieve happiness.

Live each day for itself, he had said, and don't worry about the past or the future. During the long weekend, he told them to meditate for twenty or thirty minutes every morning.

"The world is a beautiful place. You are alive. Therefore be happy."

That Sunday, Brian Epstein was found lying dead on his side with an array of pill bottles on his bedside cabinet. He was just thirty-two and he died as he lived—alone.

Within an hour of the news of Brian's death, one of the reporters assigned to stake out the Beatles' meditations was told to break the news to them. At first, the four of them could not believe it, but then the reporters told them of the pill bottles, told them that the police thought it was suicide and it all began to sound terrifying credible. (As it turned out, Brian hadn't committed suicide—a postmortem showed that he had died from the cumulative effective of bromide in the huge quantities of sleeping pills he swallowed every night.)

"I had the feeling that anybody has when somebody close to them dies," said John. "There is a sort of little hysterical, sort of hee, hee, I'm glad it's not me or something in it, the funny feeling when somebody close to you dies. I don't know whether you've had it, but I've had a lot of people die around me and the feeling is: 'What the fuck? What can I do?' I knew we were in trouble then. I didn't really have any misconceptions about our ability to do anything other than play music and I was scared. I thought: 'We've fuckin' had it.'"

The Maharishi called them in. There, surrounded by flowers, he talked to them as a parent talks to a child whose pet has just perished: clichés of Brian's journey to a better place. They should be happy and rejoice for him, the Maharishi said. Hideously, grotesquely, John began to giggle and the others, too, joined his snickering, laughing in the guilty way small children laugh when they have killed a blackbird with a chance stone from a catapult. They were no longer completely normal.

3

AFTER BRIAN EPSTEIN'S DEATH, the Beatles embarked on a brave new adventure, an adventure which brought the four closer together than they had been in a long time—the creation of Apple Corps Ltd. Apple was the culmination of a Beatle fantasy, a new way of doing business in a new age. The germ of the idea for the company had been Clive Epstein's, Brian's brother, who realized the Beatles needed a subsidiary, alternative enterprise as a tax shelter to avoid the steep British income tax.

They had finally hit upon the notion of a vast creative and commercial complex which would embrace television, literature, films, records, clothes, electronics, and anything else which was exciting and new.

"The aim of the company isn't a stack of gold teeth in the bank," said John. "We've done that bit. It's more of a trick to see if we can get artistic freedom within a business structure; to see if we can create things and sell them without charging three times our cost."

Their hippie corporation would straddle the world, benevolently doling out funds to poets, writers, inventors, musicians, and designers. All these brilliant, beautiful people would repay them by earning pots of gold for the company so they could grow larger and help still more artists. It was a visionary, wonderful idea and the four of them decided that they would become deeply involved in it themselves. At least one Beatle would see every struggling artist or poet. They had the time now, and if the supplicant showed promise they would advise and encourage—no longer would people have to go through all the trauma and cant the Beatles had had to endure before they were given the opportunity to make their first record.

One of their first Apple ventures was a lavish boutique on London's Baker Street. The outside was painted with outrageous psychedelic patterns, much to young London's delight and the neighbors' horror. The place was filmed by TV crews, photographed by newspapermen from all over the world.

Yet, curiously, the shop didn't seem to be making any money. Very rapidly, it cost the Beatles $200,000. And they began to worry. . . .

But there was so much else to occupy Apple: they sponsored Punch-and-Judy shows on Brighton Beach, and drew up plans for the launch of a new range of suits that would almost certainly prove to be as popular as collarless Beatle jackets had been only a few years earlier. They found and encouraged a brilliant new singer-songwriter, James Taylor. And then there was a group called the Iveys, later to be renamed Badfinger. Paul was bowled over when he listened to the tapes they had sent him in the plush new Apple offices on Savile Row: with their harmonies and joyous bounce, they could have been the early Beatles.

Under the Beatles' paternal guidance, they would have their first hits—"Maybe Tomorrow," "Come and Get It," and "No Matter What." Later, when they began to worry about their identity, they broke style by writing the haunting song "Without You," which would become a worldwide hit for Harry Nilsson.

During this time, Paul was using his strength to unite the Beatles in another way—by persuading them to make a new album and a film. Contrary to popular belief, he had long been stronger than John, more able. He had tried to talk to the other three about the project but they seemed so uninterested that he had sat down to work out the details with Big Mal Evans, one of the Beatles' oldest friends.

Big Mal and Neil Aspinall had both been with the Beatles since the early days. When the Beatles were in the studio, one of the two would always be there to look after them, to ensure that everything went smoothly; ready and willing to sort out any hassles.

Paul's latest project, he informed Big Mal grandly, was to be a *Magical Mystery Tour*. They would take a coachload of actors and a film crew around England with them and simply make a movie of the result. The whole thing would form a perfect backdrop to their new album.

Unfortunately for Paul, things were so badly organized without the help of Brian Epstein that every day was chaos. John and George began to bitterly resent the way in which Paul had begun to chide them and tell them what to do. They didn't like the way in which he seemed to think that he was more able than they were.

The finished film wasn't merely bad, it was a complete artistic disaster, and even the group's most committed fans found it hard to defend when it was shown on British television on the day after Christmas, 1967. Still, the movie made a profit.

In February of 1968, six months after Brian's death, the Beatles all set off to stay at Maharishi's Meditation Training Center at Reshikesh, high in the mountains of India.

There, along with many other celebrities, including the actress Mia Farrow, Mike Love of the Beach Boys, and Donovan, the English folksinger, they spent weeks learning to withdraw into themselves in meditation. Sometimes John would go into a semi-trance for days at a time, missing meals, not saying a word. But no one was that surprised because John had always possessed the strange ability to turn inward. Sometimes, at his home in Surrey, he would be happy to spend a day just sitting in a chair looking at the garden, dreaming.

Ringo and his wife, Maureen, thought the whole thing was a lot of nonsense; they hated the heat and the flies and they dashed off home after a few days to tell their friends that it had been like a cheap seaside resort. Paul, too, was less than enamored by the Indian experience, but he stuck it out longer.

Eventually, even George and John found the endless meditation becoming tiresome and they began to harbor seeds of skepticism about the Maharishi's motives. It was Magic Alex, who had traveled with them, who turned the whole thing on its head by telling George and John that his holiness had attempted to seduce the waifish Mia Farrow. At first, none of them could believe it.

"We stayed up all night discussing was it true or not true," John told *Rolling Stone*. "When George started thinking it might be true, I thought: Well, it must be true: because if George started thinking it might be true, there must be something in it. So we went to see Maharishi, the whole gang of us, the next day, charged down to his hut, his bungalow, his very rich-looking bungalow in the mountains, and as usual, when the dirty work came, I was the spokesman— whenever the dirty work came, I actually had to be leader, wherever the scene was, when it came to the nitty-gritty, I had to do the speaking—and I said: 'We're leaving.'

"'Why?' he asked, and all that shit and I said: 'Well, if you're so cosmic, you'll know why.'

"He was always intimating, and there were all these right-hand men always intimating, that he did miracles. And I said: 'You know why.'

"And he said: 'I don't know why, you must tell me.'

"And I just kept saying: 'You ought to know.' And he gave me a look like: 'I'll kill you, you bastard,' and I knew then. I had called his bluff and I was a bit rough to him."

Cynthia, though, remained convinced that the Maharishi had been misjudged: "I felt that what we were doing was wrong, very, very wrong," she said. "To sit in judgment on a man who had given us nothing but happiness . . ."

There followed a higgledy-piggledy, undignified rush to take the first flight home to England.

For the twelve months after Brian had died, and following the betrayal of their trust by the Maharishi, they had been very wobbly indeed. John, in particular, had been so angry with the Maharishi that he had written a vitriolic song accusing him of making a fool of everyone. "Maharishi, you'll get yours yet," he sang. Eventually, however, he had been pressed not to attack the Maharishi, and so had substituted the name "Sexy Sadie" instead.

The ever-widening gulf between John and Paul continued. Paul was in his late twenties, and thinking about a family.

Though Paul's relationship with Jane had certain jagged edges, the two of them had always felt they would eventually marry. On Christmas Day, 1967, he had presented her with an exquisite emerald-and-diamond engagement ring and they both told their families that they would marry in the summer. "I just want to have lots and lots of babies," said Jane. "We just want to be alone together, away from everyone."

John, meanwhile, was confused about love. He had really only married Cynthia because she was pregnant; they both knew that. Over the years, they had become bored with one another but they shared the same devotion to their son, Julian, and Cynthia gave John the stability he craved. Sometimes they talked about having more children, but mostly John was content to dream his days away.

Cynthia wasn't able to calm him, nor could the responsibilities of fatherhood, but the success and security that the Beatles represented had helped him to mellow. Still, though, he missed the giggly, intimate, lunatic relationship he had once enjoyed with his mother. Cynthia was much more serious; unlike him she wanted to be respectable, she cared what people thought. And so he spent most of his time at home with her and Julian, smoking dope and escaping

John's son, Julian

endlessly into one television program after another. Between Cynthia and Paul, he was happy—but really he wanted both of them in one package, together with a little craziness, of course. John had always liked a little craziness.

At least they had the new album to put together. After the esoteric heights of *Sgt. Pepper* and the silliness of *Magical Mystery Tour,* they determined that this record would be an honest return to basics; to the directness and intimacy of *Please, Please Me; Rubber Soul;* and *Help!*—the kind of records which had made them successful in the first place.

Their spell in India had given them a chance to think deeply about themselves for the first time and many of the songs for the new album had been written in-between long sessions of meditation. John, however, was distracted. Yoko Ono, whom he had met at an art exhibition she had given, was very much on his mind. Yoko wrote him strange, cryptic letters that made his spine tingle and set his head racing at the thought of her magic: "I'm a cloud," she'd say. "Watch for me in the sky." He would watch and then, inevitably, he would discern her face and billowing hair in the clouds above.

Though he had agreed with Paul that they would credit all their songs to Lennon and McCartney for as long as the Beatles lasted, the two of them had now completely ceased writing together and the result of this new independence, coupled with their meditation, was a deeper plumbing of their emotional depths than had ever before been possible.

Perhaps the most beautiful song to come out of the *"White Album,"* as the album came to be known, was "Julia," John's ethereal hymn to his mother. In the lyrics, John plainly laid his soul, his deepest, innermost feelings bare, and, in the process, he once again had advanced the whole of pop music.

Paul, too, was growing increasingly honest, daring for the first time to express his inner self in his lyrics.

In many ways, not writing together was proving beneficial

to them musically; certainly, they were writing some of the very best songs of their careers. But the trouble was that the fun seemed to be going out of it all, somehow.

Mainly, the others believed, it was Paul's fault. Now that they had plenty of time, they didn't need to worry about playing concerts and everything was straightforward: making the album should have been simple and unpressured. But Paul found their lackadaisical attitude maddening, he grew furious when they seemed uninterested and sloppy. He seemed to feel it was incumbent upon him to hold the band together. To a certain extent, he was justified: John had to be nagged and kicked into action or he would quite possibly have stayed at home to spend even more time smoking dope and watching TV. George had grown to hate fame so much that he was reluctant to make another album for a while because he wanted to give the fans and the newspapers a chance to become less interested in everything they did.

But, of all of them, Ringo was the most fed-up. When they did one of Paul's songs now, it was like making a record by Paul McCartney and his backing group. Much the same situation arose when they did one of John or George's songs. But, since Ringo didn't write, he found himself being shoved further and further into the background. Sometimes the others would talk for hours about what they planned to do and then just issue him his instructions at the last minute. He was scarcely involved at all, and began to feel that he no longer had any real role in the band.

His simmering temper finally exploded when, after he had been waiting all night for instructions, Paul finally told him what he wanted—then chided him because he didn't get it right the first time.

"Look, this is how you should be playing it," muttered Paul, grabbing Ringo's sticks and playing his drums for him.

"Stuff it," shouted Ringo. "If you don't like the way I play, do it yourself."

He went away for a week to think things over after that. When Paul had apologized, he finally agreed to return. Even though McCartney had smothered his drum-kit with flowers, he still felt hostile toward him.

"Paul is the greatest bass player in the world," he said later. "But he is also very determined. He goes on and on to see if he can get his own way. While that may be a virtue, it also meant that musical disagreements were inevitable."

Cynthia was worried when she returned with bronzed skin and glowing eyes from her holiday in Greece. It was four in the afternoon yet the porch lights of their house were on and the curtains were drawn. She was with her friends and they were all in high spirits. They had lunched in Rome and now they planned to drag John out for dinner in London. When Cynthia pushed the front door, it swung open. No one had bothered to lock it.

They walked through the house, calling to see if anyone was home. Eventually, Cynthia pushed open the door of the morning room to find the curtains drawn, dirty dishes heaped high on the table, and John sitting facing her in his dressing gown. With him, with her back to Cynthia, was Yoko.

"Oh, hi," they both murmured, smiling toward Cynthia. She felt her stomach churning as though she had just leapt from an airplane without a parachute, and felt a ringing in her ears.

Paul and Jane were both feeling that their relationship had gone as far as it could go. He wanted her to have babies, to give up acting, to spend all her time with him. He seemed to have somehow lost the easy intimacy he had for so long enjoyed with John and now he craved more of Jane than he had needed before.

They went to his brother Mike's wedding in June, 1968, and, on the way home, they talked of the way they had grown apart, of their different needs. It was, they both knew, over.

Jane Asher

The Fool, the boutique on Baker Street, too, was proving to be an ever-more-expensive disaster; the easygoing Apple administration was being taken ever wilder advantage of by the staff—at least one of whom admitted that she regularly used to help herself to $100 a week from the till. The Fool staff, confident in the backing of their millionaire benefactors, were spending money recklessly, ordering huge quantities of lavish clothing, and still not making money for Apple.

The Fool staff were warned in writing that they were not to take any more garments from the workshops of the company which was making them, and then, in July, 1968, all the people at the boutique were told they would have to find new jobs within two weeks as the shop was closing. Announcing their decision to the world, the Beatles said they would give all their leftover clothes away to the first people to come into the shop on its last day of business.

The Beatles were, however, a shade less generous than they appeared to be: on the night before the closure, they slipped into the shop with their friends and took away all the best clothes. Nevertheless, nearly $40,000 worth of shimmering garments were ripped away by crowds of hysterical, greedy people on the following morning.

"A bad mistake that one," said Paul—and they all agreed.

After a while, Cynthia and John got together again. The interlude was to be short-lived, however. When John went with Paul to New York on a business trip, Cynthia decided she would go to Italy for a holiday with Julian and her mother.

The holiday was restoring her confidence, making her realize that she was still a young, attractive woman. Until early one morning when she returned, singing and dancing down the street, to find a lugubrious Magic Alex waiting in the street outside her hotel.

"John is going to divorce you and take Julian away from you," he told her. "He has sent me to tell you." She couldn't quite believe this was happening to her. She became ill and stayed in bed in Italy for several weeks. On her return to London, she found a divorce petition waiting for her. In it John accused her of adultery. It was the ultimate ignominy. . . .

Paul, meanwhile, was still in love with the Beatles. He felt confused and slightly lost.

Sometimes, late at night when the mood struck him, he would open the window of his huge house in St. John's Wood to play and sing quietly for the "scruffs"—the devoted girl fans who were forever hanging around outside his high wooden front gate.

Paul's mansion in St. Johns Woods, London

There was something touching and just a little forlorn about the millionaire sitting alone in his castle singing "Blackbird" or "Yesterday" to anyone who would listen.

Shortly afterward, however, Paul had a new girlfriend—photographer Linda Eastman, whom he had met a year previously in New York. Paul found himself talking long into the night with Linda's father, Lee Eastman, about Apple's problems.

Neil Aspinall was struggling desperately to halt Apple's disintegration. No decisions could be made without the consent of all four Beatles, and persuading them to consent to even talk to one another was becoming difficult.

Floating high on their cloud of love, John and Yoko seemed scarcely to notice the shouts of "Nip!" and "Get back to your own country!" that the fans yelled at her in the street. So cocooned were they that they seemed to look upon the calls as joking gestures of affection. Once, as they went into Apple, one of the "scruffs" handed Yoko a raggedy cluster of yellow roses—thorns first, so they would prick her hands and make them bleed. "Thank you," John beamed. "It's about time somebody made Yoko feel welcome around here."

"You," Yoko had once told John, after gazing long into his eyes, "are *sanpaku*." *Sanpaku*, she explained patiently, was a Japanese term meaning, literally, "three whites." If a person was *sanpaku*, it meant that the irises of their eyes were turned upward so that white could be seen on three sides. The condition had been recognized for centuries in Oriental countries and it was known to signify poor physical and psychological health—caused primarily by an unwholesome diet. Worse, people who were *sanpaku* were prone to meet with violent accidents or death. "Look," she had said, showing him photographs. "President Kennedy was not *sanpaku* in his younger, dynamic years. But shortly before his assassination, he became *sanpaku*. Hitler, too, was *sanpaku* before his death. History showed Julius Caesar,

Abraham Lincoln, and dozens more had become *sanpaku* toward the end of their lives." The two of them had pored together over photographs of the Beatles and realized that, though none of them had been *sanpaku* in their early days, now they all were. John was not surprised. He had believed inwardly for a while that the Beatles were a spent force, that their continued existence was an unhealthy pretense.

The ivory phone rang urgently in the office of Neil Aspinall, Apple's managing director, on October 18, 1968; it was John calling. "Imagine your worst paranoia, Neil, because it's here right now. We've been busted."

They had been warned three weeks before by a Fleet Street show business journalist that the police were out to get them but neither of them had really believed it was possible, they had been untouchable for so long. But at midday on October 18, as John and Yoko lay making love in the basement flat, there had come hammering at the door. Yoko had made a dash for the bathroom to slip a dress on while John fumbled around, searching for his trousers. John reluctantly opened the front door, and the tiny flat was filled suddenly with policemen and policewomen.

A policeman found a small ball of marijuana, fastidiously wrapped in silver paper in a binocular case. More dope was found in an envelope in an old suitcase.

"OK," said John. "The dope all belongs to me. It's nothing to do with Yoko."

John was fined nearly $400 for possessing 219 grains of marijuana. "The way things are going," John would be moved to write soon afterwards, "they're gonna crucify me. . . ."

4

AT THE TIME that the Beatles were completing their filming and recording of *Get Back,* Stephen Maltz, Apple's bright young accountant, was desperately struggling to place some kind of control on the company's spending. So far all his pleas to the Beatles had been ignored. Finally he was driven to resign with a letter to his employers which spelled out the dire financial consequences of their dilettanteism: "You have houses and you have cars but you also have serious court cases pending with the Inland Revenue which could leave you with very little indeed." He also told them that if Apple was not drastically reorganized, they would inevitably be driven into insolvency.

Characteristically, John immediately dashed out to give a string of interviews in which he told the world of Apple's financial morass. "I'm broke—down to my last £50,000," he said.

In New York, Allen Klein read the reports and smiled to himself like a fox spying a particularly plump and unsuspecting rabbit.

Klein had been the manager of the Rolling Stones since 1965 and in that time had dramatically increased their royalty rate so that they were earning more than the Beatles—even though they sold fewer records.

After a series of transatlantic phone calls, he finally

Allen Klein

persuaded John and Yoko to meet him in his suite at the plush Dorchester Hotel on London's Park Lane.

To their delight, they found Klein to be a cuddly, amiable bear of a man who wore an old sweater and seemed to be every bit as nervous as they were. What's more, he had done his homework; he talked with John about the Beatles' songs, seemed genuinely interested and intrigued by everything they had done. He also bubbled with ideas to help them sort out their finances. "You realize that your records account for half of EMI's music profits around the world and yet they still pay you a ridiculous ten percent royalty," he told them. "We've got to change that. From now on those guys should be paying you at least a twenty-five percent royalty."

When John had gasped in disbelief, Klein told him: "Don't worry—they need you more than you need them."

"He's like a poker player," John said to Yoko later. "And he is either going to bluff his way through and win and everything will be wonderful. Or he will lose and then we have all had it."

By the end of the evening, John was sold and at Klein's suggestion, he wrote to Sir Joseph Lockwood, the head of EMI: "Dear Sir Joe, from now on Allen Klein handles all my stuff."

The poker player had won his first hand. Now he met with the other three and told them that he didn't want them to pay him a penny unless he helped them to earn more money.

"Look," he said. "All I'm asking for is twenty percent of any *extra* money I earn for you—that's how certain I am that you are missing out on millions upon millions of pounds you should be receiving. . . ."

George and Ringo both signed promptly but Paul wanted to wait until he could talk things over with Lee Eastman. Klein seemed straightforward enough, but there was something about his bald aggressiveness which made Paul feel uneasy. . . .

Linda Eastman, Paul discovered, was pregnant. Paul had been taken slightly aback when she had first told him, but not for long. He asked Linda to marry him.

Paul was ready for the family life. He adored Linda's little daughter Heather so much that he had invited her along to dance in the studio during the January film sessions of *Get Back*. He liked the idea of a house filled with laughter and playing children. The familial picture seemed so idyllic and complete.

George and Patti would have liked children, as well, but somehow none had come along. The absence of babies seemed to place a strain on their marriage so that, though they loved one another, they would sometimes argue furious-

ly over trivial things. Once she had collected dozens of pairs
of old spectacles for a charity which sent them to nearsighted
people in Africa. The charity had been so pleased they had
arranged for the *Daily Mirror* to write a little piece about
Patti's generosity. George had flown into a rage when he read
it. Though he was the most generous of all the Beatles, he
hated it when the newspapers found out about his bene-
volence.

Sometimes, when Patti really wanted to annoy George, she
flirted with his best friend, Eric Clapton. Eric had played
guitar with George on the Beatles' song "While My Guitar
Gently Weeps" and George rated him as the finest guitarist in
Britain. Before George married, he had once stolen one of
Eric's girlfriends away and the guitarist had always felt a
vague resentment, a faint desire to get even. And so Eric and
Patti delighted in flirting blatantly in front of George. For the
most part, however, when the three of them got together,
they would simply roll huge joints and quietly smoke
themselves insensible.

On March 12, 1969, on a day that emphasized how distant
the four Beatles had become, in a large garishly painted
house on Cavendish Avenue, St. John's Wood, a newly clean-
shaven Paul McCartney slipped into his smartest dark suit
and whitest shirt for his wedding day.

Linda had dashed down to Marylebone Register Office on
the previous day to give notice of their plan to plight their
troth. Paul, meanwhile, was concerned with far more serious
matters: he was busy producing the new Jackie Lomax
single, "Thumbin' a Ride," for Apple. So busy, indeed, that he
forgot to buy Linda a wedding ring. Luckily, he managed
to persuade a local jeweler to specially open his shop
that evening so he could purchase a plain, gold ring for
about $30.

The rest of the Beatles were noticeable only by their
absence. None of them had been invited—primarily because
they now disliked Paul so much that they probably wouldn't
have come.

The whole of Fleet Street seemed to be at the ceremony, however, and afterwards Paul invited them back to the house to sip champagne and ask impertinent questions.

"No," said Linda for the thousandth time. "I've nothing to do with the Eastman Kodak family."

"What?" grimaced Paul. "I've been done. Where's the money?"

The girls who hung around Paul's front gate day and night hated Linda. They had booed and hissed her when she and Paul returned after the wedding. Linda just couldn't deal with the "scruffs" at all, tending to treat them as though they were rivals for Paul's affections.

On the same day, meanwhile, the drug squad of Scotland Yard was searching for George Harrison's house. They knew where they were going: a modern bungalow called Kinfauns which was supposed to be on a private estate owned by the National Trust. But the estate was so skillfully designed that all the houses were hidden by shrubbery. The only way to find each building was to look for little nameplates set at regular distances in the shrubbery. Shrewdly, George had removed his nameplate as soon as he moved in.

Eventually, after nearly an hour of searching, the police managed to find the house by a process of elimination. Even without the nameplate, one look at the building convinced them they had arrived at their destination, for the whole place had been sprayed with yellow, red, and purple psychedelic patterns. It was late now, about 7:30 in the evening, and Patti was reluctant to open the door because George was up in London at the recording studio. The policemen showed her their search warrant, however, and they entered, looking curiously around them; they were as interested as anyone else in seeing how a Beatle lived. They looked at the huge heated swimming pool, admired the floor-to-ceiling circular windows overlooking the landscaped gardens, and then suggested gently that perhaps Patti should phone George so they could talk with him.

"No, there is nothing there," George told the detective

nervously on the phone. "There is only the stuff I got on prescription on top of the fridge."

Of course, George being George, the police found dope hidden in almost every room. When they had finished their search, Patti made them a nice pot of tea and they sat down on the floor cushions beside the low Oriental tables to listen to Beatle records, watch TV, and chat. When George tiptoed tremulously through the door, they arrested him. The couple was subsequently fined almost $600 each at Esher and Walton Magistrates Court.

Eight days after Paul and George's busy day, John and Yoko, also without the attendance of the other Beatles, were married in Gibraltar. They hadn't really planned for the ceremony to take place on that particular barren rock—they had wanted a ship's captain to marry them. But the ship captains they had approached—especially the ones on the cross-channel car ferries—had looked at them askance and told them they were no longer empowered to do that kind of thing. To marry in Paris or Berlin would have taken ages. And so they chose Gibraltar.

Just when the world's press was desperately trying to find out where they had vanished to, John and Yoko resurfaced in Suite 902 of the Amsterdam Hilton with an invitation to journalists and photographers everywhere to join them on their honeymoon. The invitation was widely misconstrued and the first reporters to creep awkwardly into the room seemed to expect John and Yoko to make love in front of them. Instead, the pair of them sat up in bed and began talking very seriously about the immorality of the war and how if everyone worked together there would be peace throughout the world. Inevitably, the papers lampooned them mercilessly. "But we knew they would," John said later. "Anyway, it's better to have a couple of clowns on the front pages making people laugh and talking about peace than to have the usual pictures of tricky politicians and warmongers shaking people's hands." Certainly the bed-in was more comprehensible than the bagism event the couple had staged at the Albert Hall a few months previously. That simply consisted of the two of them writhing about on stage in a huge white bag.

The bed-in lasted for seven days, during which time John and Yoko held court for the world's media from ten in the morning until ten at night.

A few days later, they flew to Vienna for the premiere of their film *Rape,* a shocking movie vastly different from John and Yoko's earlier films, which consisted of John smiling or gradually achieving an erection. For *Rape,* a film crew was instructed to simply follow the first pretty young woman they saw, with their camera and sound recorder running. The gradual shift in the girl's attitude—from glee, to amusement, to nervousness and terror as she found it impossible to escape the crew—reflected the pressure John had been under from the media, he said.

At Apple, Allen Klein had begun a purge of the company's personnel. Clearly, some of the people Klein was disposing of were not productive, but some, like Peter Asher, were enormously talented young men who had earned hundreds of thousands of pounds for Apple. Klein's policy appeared to be simply to destroy anyone who in any way threatened to come between him and the Beatles. The band themselves studiously avoided the pleas of their employees, many of whom had been friends since their schooldays together in Liverpool. John, especially, seemed to feel they had it coming to them because they had been so cool with Yoko. But there was something even more unpleasant in the way in which the other three so easily dropped their idealism and their dreams of universal brotherly love when they began to prove expensive. Like feudal monarchs, they seemed happy to condone the expedient execution of their faithful retainers while closing their ears to all pleas for mercy.

John and Yoko bought a vast white Georgian mansion set among seventy-four acres of rolling parkland just outside Ascot. The historic building, called Tittenhurst Park, cost over $300,000. He changed his name to John Ono Lennon in an official legal ceremony on the roof of Apple. During this time, he made a Beatles' single called "The Ballad of John and Yoko." Since Ringo was away acting in a film called *The Magic Christian* and George was busy making a record with a London sect of Rhada Krishna monks, Paul had played bass, drums, and had sung harmonies while John had overdubbed himself on guitar. Musically, they could still do no wrong.

John and Yoko with accused murderer Michael X, for whose cause the Lennons relentlessly, if unsuccessfully, campaigned. Michael X was later convicted and hanged

John and Yoko decided to take their peace campaign to the United States to crystallize youthful outrage against the Vietnam war. The paranoid Nixon administration had decided that they were subversive, however, so John's application for a visa was stalled . . . and stalled . . . and stalled.

"OK," said John. "We'll go as near as we can to the States and do the bed-in there for the American media. They won't mind flying out to see us."

They eventually moved their entourage and their peace posters to the Queen Elizabeth Hotel in Montreal. Once again John noticed the marked difference in attitude toward him between England and the States. Where the British reporters had only mocked, their American counterparts listened solemnly to his words. He spoke for hours on the phone to radio stations all over America and phone-ins with their audiences showed that, perhaps because America was weary of the longest war in her history, young people were receptive to his ideas, eager to follow his initiative.

In between the interviews, John had written an anthem for his campaign which he decided to record from his and Yoko's bed. They invited a host of friends—including acid's high priest Timothy Leary with his wife Rosemary, comedian Tommy Smothers, a rabbi, and the Canadian chapter of the Rhada Krishna Temple—to join them on the record and thus was born the song which was to become a rallying call for oppressed people throughout the globe . . . "Give Peace a Chance."

After Canada, John and Yoko went with Yoko's daughter, Kyoko, for a driving holiday in Scotland to recharge their batteries after the rigors of their Canadian bed-in. Unfortunately, John had not driven a car for years and he had never liked cars much—he didn't even pass his driving test until he was twenty-four.

Inevitably, he had driven their rented Austin Maxi into a ditch and they had all three been hauled off to a hospital. John, who was the most seriously hurt, needed seventeen stitches while Yoko received fourteen and Kyoko, four.

The twenty-nine hours of tapes from the January session were still gathering dust. None of them could face the terrifying job of trying to edit the whole miserable mess into an album. So they had decided to go back to St. John's Wood to put together a completely new LP which they planned to simply call *Abbey Road*. On the first morning, when they arrived in the studio, Yoko had brought in a camp bed because she had hurt her back in the car accident. For the other three Beatles, it was the final straw: bringing your old lady along to a recording session was bad enough but to bring her bed as well was ridiculous. John sensed their resentment and rapidly lost interest in the whole project. Paul, too, was trying so hard not to upset anyone that his work became insipid as a result.

So, curiously, it was left to George, the young apprentice come of age, to dominate the album with two superlative songs—"Something," a love song to Patti, and "Here Comes the Sun," a number he had been inspired to write while sitting in Eric's garden.

George Martin remembers the sessions as being miserable. It was obvious to him and to the Beatles themselves that they were falling apart. George, like John, had had enough of being a Beatle: "I feel as though all that is far behind me," he said. "It all seems so trivial, it doesn't matter any more—none of it. What I am interested in now is finding out the answers to the real questions, the things which really matter in life. . . ." Paul alone still seemed to love the band, still tried to coax the other three into recapturing the magic.

The Sixties seemed to be taking a bad turn. The world was just beginning to hear vague rumors of children starving to death in a faraway, unheard-of land called Biafra. And Britain had sent troops to Belfast in an effort to control a rapidly deteriorating situation.

America was in the eighth year of its bloody war in Vietnam: a war in which America had been rendered impotent despite its technological might, a war in which 34,000 American young men had been needlessly slaughtered.

The Beatles, who had grown and then flowered with the Sixties, seemed to be withering and dying with the decade. In Prague, Paris, London, and Washington, there was a smoldering resentment which intermittently flashed into flame.

On July 2, 1969, Brian Jones dropped a lot of downers, then drank far too much vodka. Hazily, he swam across his pool. The night was very dark and he was very alone. Jones

Brian Jones

was still despondent over being kicked out of the Rolling Stones. The Beatles were not the only people who were finding it hard to come to terms with the after-the-party mood of the end of the Sixties. . . . In the early morning of July 3, Brian was found dead in his swimming pool.

Charles Manson had seen the race riots throughout the U.S., felt the mood of anger and bitterness that was seething throughout the black communities. Through his curious reading of the *Book of Revelations,* he became convinced that a race war had been preordained by God in order to precipitate Armageddon, the day of judgment. More, he now believed implicitly that he had been chosen to lead the way out of the chaos that was to come and to eventually restore sanity and a new order to the world.

The Beatles were not simply pop musicians to him; they were prophets, possessed of supernormal powers. Their songs had mystical significance. Their "White Album" was the last record they would make; it was a prelude to global warfare. Every song on the record reinforced his belief. The broken-winged blackbird learning to fly in "Blackbird" was a symbol of the black people of the world, who must arise and destroy the white man.

In George Harrison's song "Piggies," the Beatles couldn't be more explicit. The time was ripe for black militants to rise up and give the white "pigs" the "damn good whacking" they had had coming to them for years.

The means to overthrow the pigs was spelled out in John Lennon's song "Happiness is a Warm Gun." Susan Atkins, whom Manson had had sex with and taken on LSD trips, had been rechristened Sadie Mae Glutz. Manson was not surprised to discover a song on the "White Album" entitled "Sexy Sadie."

Manson interpreted "Rocky Raccoon," "Revolution #1," and "Revolution #9," in the same way. "Revolution #9," particularly, with its discordant noises, whispers, screams, musical anarchy, and the word "rise" repeated twice, symbolized to Manson the sounds of the coming holocaust. It was the blueprint for Armageddon.

Manson believed that "Helter Skelter" was the code name for the war. He had no idea that a helter-skelter is simply a special type of slide which has long been an integral part of every British fun fair.

In August of 1969, four members of Charles Manson's family stopped their car outside the front gates of a large and imposing mansion. One of them deftly climbed a telegraph pole to sever telephone wires.

Like a highly trained team of Green Berets, they slid over the high security fence surrounding the house. As they made to hide their bundles of clothing in the surrounding shrubbery, they saw a flash of headlights and heard the sound of a car crunching along the driveway toward them, away from the house.

The youth leading the intruders flagged the car down with the word "Halt."

He pointed a gun directly at the driver's face as the confused teen-ager pleaded: "Please don't hurt me. I won't say anything."

His begging turned to a piercing scream as the sound of four gunshots rent the still of the night.

As Manson's followers made their way into the main living room of the house, they woke the Polish playboy Voytek Frykowski, who had been sleeping on a couch. In his drowsy state, the man appeared to mistake the trio for friends and he asked them the time.

"Who are you and what are you doing here?" asked Frykowski, his voice trembling.

"I am the Devil and I am here to do the Devil's business," the boy snarled.

Pulling out butcher-sharp knives, Manson's girls stalked the house.

The most striking of the four captives they took was Sharon Tate, an actress who was best known for her appearance in the film *Valley of the Dolls*.

Also taken captive, besides Frykowski, were Jay Sebring and Abigail "Gibby" Folger.

"You are all going to die," one of their captors told them calmly.

Pandemonium broke out as Frykowski, Sharon Tate, and Gibby Folger fought for their lives. When it was over, Sharon had been stabbed sixteen times, Jay had been shot dead and then stabbed seven times, Gibby had been stabbed twenty-eight times and Frykowski had been shot twice, stabbed fifty-one times and struck over the head with a blunt object thirteen times.

As the four lay dying, one of the killers dipped a towel into Sharon Tate's blood and wrote the word "PIG" in blood on a door. . . .

Helter Skelter had begun.

One major impetus for the Beatles' final break-up, though none of them knew it at the time, began with an innocuous call to John in September of 1969 from a concert promoter in Toronto. He had assembled all of rock 'n' roll's great original stars—people like Jerry Lee Lewis and Chuck Berry—for a festival on the following day and he would be happy to pay for seven return tickets to Toronto for John and his friends if they would simply attend the show.

"OK," said John, his eyes sparkling at the chance of performing without the rest of the Beatles. "We'll come. But only if you let me bring my new band so we can play. . . ."

John ordered Anthony Fawcett, his right-hand man, to get him Eric Clapton, Klaus Voorman, "and that new drummer we were listening to, Alan White—and tell Mal he's coming to organize everything."

But by the next morning, no one had been able to contact Clapton, although messages had been left for him all over the southeast of England. Without Eric, John seemed to suffer a change of heart, complaining that Yoko didn't feel well and he thought they should cancel.

But then a startled Eric Clapton received a call from one of John's aides telling him about the show.

"John just sits there and thinks up these things you wouldn't believe," Eric recalled later. "I just had a phone call on the day we were to leave and he said that someone had asked him to do that concert and it was that night! So I had to make the airport in an hour."

Eric's enthusiasm rubbed off on John, and John set off for the airport, prepared to teach his new "band" their songs on the flight across the Atlantic. By the time they arrived at the airport, a huge, curious crowd had gathered and a limousine was waiting to whisk them straight to the Varsity Stadium. As the car slipped into the arena, John's hands were shaking, and he was feeling more nervous than he had ever felt in his life. There he was about to perform the first show he had ever played without the Beatles and he wasn't even sure which songs he was going to sing. He had a band he had never worked with and he couldn't remember the lyrics to anything except his new Beatle songs.

As the band began warming up for a quick practice session backstage, he was so overwhelmed by fear that he vomited repeatedly in a corner of the dressing room while the other musicians looked away, embarrassed to see the man they revered as a demigod suddenly so childlike and vulnerable. Even now he was scrabbling for excuses not to go on. But Eric took him by the arm and led him out into the glare of the lights and the avalanche roar of a crowd who loved him; then somehow they were stumbling into Presley's classic "Blue Suede Shoes," and the old Beatles' songs "Money" and "Dizzy Miss Lizzie."

"What's next?" John screamed at Eric, suddenly lost. "Yer Blues," he was told; then they followed with two new numbers, "Cold Turkey" and "Give Peace a Chance."

"I couldn't remember any of the words, but it didn't

matter—I just made them all up and we made a great, wonderful noise," he said. After the show, Carl Perkins, the veteran rock 'n' roll star and one of John's earliest heroes, came up to John and whispered in his ear: "You were so beautiful you made me cry."

At Apple a week later, John was still feeling euphoric.

"Look, now that you are back into performing again, why don't we do a TV show or something?" asked Paul, who would have given his eye teeth to have played the Toronto gig.

"No," said John.

"Well how about us just doing one big gig as the Beatles?"

"No," John repeated.

"Well, all right then, why don't we just go out under a false name and play little village halls just for the hell of it."

"Look," said John, staring murderously into Paul's face, his eyes bright pinpoints of light. "I think you're daft. I'm leaving the Beatles. I want a divorce."

5

THOUGH HE HAD KNOWN deep inside for months that the split with John was coming, just as a couple approaching divorce know that the final break is inevitable, Paul could still not believe that it had happened. He had first played guitar with John when he was fourteen, shortly after his mother had died. They had grown up together, talked about making love to their first girls together. Together they had written their first awkward songs, learned how to excite an audience, and had evolved into the most successful songwriting duo since Gilbert and Sullivan. For many, many years, Paul thought, they had truly loved one another.

Yet some of the things John had said after announcing that he was quitting had cut Paul until he bled: that Paul had been destroying his self-confidence ever since Paul had presented him with a virtually completed *Magical Mystery Tour*. "Partly, it was my own fault," John told him. "I got this idea on acid that I had to destroy my own ego, so I went along where you pushed me, but I've been trying to tell you I want to leave for years. I just haven't had the guts to say it." John had been ashamed to be associated with many of Paul's songs, whimsical things like "Maxwell's Silver Hammer" and "Hello, Goodbye." He had fumed inwardly but said nothing when Paul had repeatedly bullied his own songs to the "A" sides of their singles.

Paul tried to explain to him that he had only been pushy because he felt that John had lost interest, that there would have been no Beatles' records at all after Brian's death if he had waited for John to snap out of his stoned dream and begin creating again. But John refused to listen; he simply wrapped his arm around Yoko, turned his back, and walked away. With one brutal swipe, John had shattered the shaky foundations of Paul's life. Quite simply, Paul could not imagine life without the Beatles.

And yet the world knew nothing of the split. *Abbey Road* had received rave reviews and was fast becoming the best-selling Beatles' album of all time. In a world where the fantasy and euphoria of the Sixties were fast beginning to collide with the gritty reality of the coming decade, the Beatles were reminders of the time, just a few short years before, when the world had been a happier, simpler place.

Allen Klein—John, George, and Ringo's manager—had asked John not to say anything about his decision: there were so many intricate business deals being juggled in the air that the slightest hint of a Beatle break-up would have cost them millions, he said. Besides he still believed, just possibly, that John could be prevailed upon to change his mind.

On his farm in Scotland, Paul lost himself in the only way he know how: writing songs. After arranging for a primitive, four-track recording studio to be installed in his house in St. John's Wood, he had flown home with his family to record. One of the first numbers he worked out seemed to be almost a subconscious response to John's noisy proclamation of his love for Yoko—it was a song called, simply, "The Lovely Linda." Frantically, Paul played drums, bass, steel guitar, electric organ, and every other instrument he had lying around the house, pouring his energy into making music just as he had after his mother died. He knew intuitively, from his years of experience with the Beatles, that at least two of the numbers—the brutally honest "Maybe I'm Amazed" and the forlorn "Every Night"—were surefire hits.

"Maybe John was right," he seemed to reason. "Maybe the

Beatles have had their day. The sooner I get this album out and get it over with, the better. . . ."

In November, 1969, John decided the time had come to make use of his M.B.E. He and Yoko typed out a letter to the Queen, with a copy to Harold Wilson. "Your Majesty," it read, "I am returning the M.B.E. in protest against Britain's involvement in the Nigeria-Biafra thing, against our support of America in Vietnam, and against 'Cold Turkey' slipping down the charts. With love, John Lennon of Bag."

John said that he had mentioned "Cold Turkey" as a joke, to take away pomposity from his gesture. The remark was a serious mistake which tended to make ridiculous an otherwise meaningful and thought-provoking statement. The Queen's spokesmen reacted with tolerant amusement, as though humoring a recalcitrant child, and the press treated the whole event as yet another madcap stunt by the Beatle who had flipped his lid. Nevertheless, there were many who recognized the sincerity behind John's move, among them veteran peace campaigner Bertrand Russell. He wrote an effusive letter of congratulation which moved John deeply.

The return of the M.B.E. was merely one of a whirlwind of stunts which John and Yoko were staging at this time. They sent acorns to Ho Chi Minh, Mao Tse-tung, and every other world leader they could think of with the suggestion that they should watch them grow for peace. They financed a poster campaign and a film calling for a Queen's pardon for James Hanratty, who had been hanged for committing rape and murder on a highway seven years before.

Several years earlier, Delaney Bramlett and Bonnie Lynn had formed a duo which made some of the most exciting gospel-tinged rock 'n' roll of their time. When the two of them asked a few of their friends to join them on a concert tour of Britain, Eric Clapton had been among those who were genuinely delighted to take up the invitation. News that Clapton was on the tour insured packed houses everywhere Delaney and Bonnie played. But few of the fans who stamped their feet and cheered with every song recognized the gaunt rhythm guitarist who played hidden behind lank hair, a huge beard, and buckskins: a very different George Harrison from the hesitant, boyish-faced mop-top who had stood on stage with the Beatles four years before was making his comeback. By mid-December, George had so recovered his confidence, so forgotten the primal fear he had experienced on the first night he joined the tour, that he was actually pleased when John phoned him one evening at Kinfauns to ask if he would join him for a peace gig he was playing at the Lyceum in London.

George arrived at the Lyceum with Delaney and Bonnie; Eric Clapton; the Who's drummer, Keith Moon; keyboard player Billy Preston; and several other illustrious friends. The entire ballroom had been plastered by John's aides with posters which screamed: "WAR IS OVER IF YOU WANT IT. LOVE, JOHN AND YOKO."

Not the least of George's motives for playing the show was his desire to close the gulf which had opened between him and John since Yoko's arrival. George had thought at first that Yoko was a ruthlessly ambitious woman who was cold-bloodedly using John for her own ends and he had tried, as best he could, to warn John of what was happening.

John had responded angrily, had refused even to speak to George for weeks afterward. Now, backstage, when John told him that Yoko would be joining them on stage, George had smiled through gritted teeth and said how delighted he was. At first, Yoko sat quietly in a white bag by John's feet while the band powered through his tortured new song, "Cold Turkey." But when they started the next number, a song dedicated to Yoko's daughter called "Don't Worry, Kyoko," she had leapt out of the bag to scream murderously at the audience, and, as the song built to a climax, she began crying: "Hanratty was innocent!" and "You killed Hanratty!"

George looked on in thinly veiled horror. After just two numbers, the band staggered off stage while the audience screamed for more. It was, said John later, the beginning of the Plastic Ono Band.

The following morning, John and Yoko boarded a jet for Toronto. They didn't want to stay in a hotel this time so arrangements had been made for them to live at the farmhouse of veteran rock 'n' roll singer Ronnie Hawkins and his wife, Wanda. Hawkins's backing group had recently split to work with Bob Dylan as the Band, so he was ecstatic at all the wonderful publicity John and Yoko's stay would bring to his comeback. When the pair arrived with an entourage which included a pair of macrobiotic cooks, two journalists, and assorted hangers-on, Ronnie's smile, to his everlasting credit, dimmed only slightly. He gave the happy couple his own bed and hadn't even murmured when a crack squad of engineers arrived from the telephone company to install a dozen extra lines in the house.

There followed a much prepublicized television interview with Marshall McLuhan, the Canadian author and media analyst, at Toronto University.

John, who hadn't bothered to read any of McLuhan's books began the interview frivolously by beaming: "How yer doin', Mr. McLuhan?"

But, as McLuhan began to talk about the beauty and immediacy of the Beatles' music, John began to warm to him: "Trying to talk about the music we make is like trying to describe a dream," he said, adding mischievously, "The Beatles are like an ancient monument—they should be changed or scrapped. . . ."

Still, John could not bring himself to confirm the break-up. It was as though he liked to feel that, whatever had happened, they were still there behind him, a bedrock of security.

John also used the program to warn young people not to experiment with drugs, a sudden change in attitude which startled many of his friends. It also led some of his more cynical contemporaries to wonder if he was perhaps trying to placate the United States immigration officials who were still refusing to grant him a visa, ostensibly because he had been convicted of possessing cannabis. John's statement was widely reported, however, and that night a call came through to the Hawkinses' farmhouse asking John if he would be prepared to give advice to a government commission which had been set up to decide whether cannabis should be made legal in Canada.

John and Yoko were ecstatic. At last all their months of toil were beginning to pay off; they were being taken seriously, people here understood their message, realized that they were formidable intellectuals not, as the British seemed to think, "two gurus in drag."

They became even more jubilant later that night when a call came through for them from Ottawa: President Trudeau would like to meet them. To John and Yoko, it was the realization of their ultimate dream: a major world leader was asking them for the benefit of their advice. Never did they consider that Trudeau, politician that he was, might want to use their popularity in exactly the same way as Harold Wilson had used the popularity of the Beatles when he presented them with M.B.E. medals five years earlier.

With customary panache, John and Yoko decided not to fly from Toronto to Ottawa, instead they would charter their own train, "like the Queen does."

The journey took three days, as they occasionally halted regally to give press conferences or to broadcast words of wisdom to ever-more sycophantic Canadian journalists. In Montreal, representatives of the government's drug commission actually came to the train so that John could sit in a siding beatifically pronouncing his views on narcotics. Back-pedaling slightly from the stance he had taken with McLuhan, John told them he thought that marijuana should be legalized, but that heroin, LSD and even pep pills were insidious and should be outlawed. Quite why the drug commission felt that a multimillionaire pop star living a remote, insulated life should be able to seriously advise them was not explained. But the meeting was symbolic of the way in which John was becoming revered as a formidable radical intellectual throughout Canada and the U.S.

At another press conference along the way, John announced that he would be playing at a huge rock festival for peace near Toronto the following July. Many other rock 'n' roll superstars would be performing, John told journalists, and they would be helping to organize a vast petition signed by tens of millions of young people around the globe calling upon President Nixon to withdraw American forces from Vietnam.

John had been so nervous the night before the meeting with President Trudeau that he had been unable to sleep, and he arrived at the president's office looking bleary-eyed and slightly wrecked, despite his immaculate new suit, white shirt, and tie. John, Yoko, and the president talked for nearly an hour about youth culture, drugs, and the generation gap. If John had felt a little uneasy when the president insisted on posing with his arms draped around John and Yoko for a blitz of camera flashes, he didn't show it. He was also happy to tell a room full of reporters, invited by the president, just how sensitive, intelligent, and altogether wonderful their president was.

"If there were more leaders like President Trudeau, there would be no more wars," he told them.

Back in London John seemed weary, so exhausted in fact that not even the news that he had been named as one of the most influential men of the decade by a BBC television program seemed to cheer him. Unknown to his friends, he had been arguing bitterly with Yoko. The drive and ambition which she was channeling through him had worn thin. He felt his triumphs had amply vindicated him in spite of the ridicule that had been heaped upon him, and he had decided he could not cope with any more peace campaigning. "Look, I'm a musician, not a politician," he had shouted at one point.

They had decided then to see the New Year in in

Denmark, at the little cabin where Yoko's ex-husband, film producer Tony Cox, was living with their daughter, Kyoko.

John, Paul, and George had been on Ringo for ages to make a solo album. But he couldn't write songs and he certainly couldn't sing very well, and he could hardly make a record of drum solos.

He talked the problem over with his mother and his stepfather as they sipped tea one afternoon in the lavish bungalow he had bought them in the posh Liverpool suburb of Woolton. Ringo's mother suggested that, as he had such a lovely voice, he should make a long-player of all those delightful old classic songs like "Whispering Grass" and "Have I Told You Lately That I Love You." Nobody had come up with a better idea, and so Ringo set to work on an album which was to be titled *Sentimental Journey*.

"All it proved," commented a reviewer for *New Musical Express* later as he gently slid the knife, "was that few people were less well-fitted to sing that material than Ringo, and everybody already knew that."

Ringo wasn't too ruffled. He knew that if he had a talent besides drumming, it was acting. After a small part in the film *Candy,* he was later to receive rave reviews when he starred opposite Peter Sellers in *The Magic Christian.*

The peace festival belonged to a part of John's life which was now over. He wanted nothing more to do with it. As a result, he told the promoters that he would not appear at the concert unless people could come to see it for nothing. Without the income from tickets, he knew it would be impossible for them to raise the finances necessary to build a stage, rent land, erect lavatories, and to do all the million-and-one other things which would have to be done if the show was not to end in even greater catastrophe than the concert the Rolling Stones had played at Altamont, California. The promoters were furious—John had never before suggested that the show should be free. Yet, though the cancellation was entirely John's fault, he later would ironically emerge as a champion of the people, while the two promoters ended up with egg all over their faces.

The album the Beatles had recorded the previous January still lay on the shelves at Apple, although hundreds of thousands of pounds' worth of their money was tied up in it. All they had really decided was that they should change the title from Paul's optimistic *Get Back* to the conclusive *Let It Be*.

Painstaking production had been an intrinsic part of the creation of all the later Beatle albums. But this time, none of the Beatles wanted anything to do with the project. They had simply dismissively asked their startled engineer, Glyn Johns, to put together the best forty minutes he could find into an album. When the resultant tape had arrived, each of them had listened to it with growing feelings of despondency. Of all of them, John had been alone in wishing the tape to be released as an LP: "I had thought it would be good to let the shitty version out," he said later, "because it would break the Beatles, break the myth. It would be just us, with no trousers on and no glossy paint over the cover, and no hype. 'This is what we are like with our trousers off. Would you please end the game now?'"

It was then that Phil Spector, the producer who has towered over the development of rock music like a Colossus, made it known that, more than anything in the world, he wished to work with the Beatles.

Spector, an unassuming boyish figure dressed from head to toe in denims, had achieved his first international success when he was the eighteen-year-old driving force behind a group called the Teddy Bears, who had a huge hit with "To Know Him Is to Love Him." From then on, he was associated with literally dozens of classic hits, from the Shirelles' "Will

You Still Love Me Tomorrow" to the Righteous Brothers' "You've Lost That Lovin' Feelin'."

The Beatles decided to give him his chance. Spector, gleefully seizing the challenge, locked himself away in a studio, intent on listening to the twenty-nine wretched hours of tape again and again. He was confident, he said, that he could make the album work.

In the midst of his toil, Spector received a frantic call from John: "Come over to Apple quick," he told him. "I've just written a monster." John had simply woken up that morning at Tittenhurst Park with the words to a song called "Instant Karma" whirling around inside his head. He dashed to Apple, determined to work out the details of the number and to record it that day while it was still fresh in his mind. When he discovered there was no piano at the office, a chauffeur had been majestically dispatched to: "Buy the best grand piano in the shop and tell them to get it here right away."

The piano was installed within an hour—mentioning a Beatle name was still the next best thing to magic. John bashed out the final details of the melody, working out the remaining lyrics and then, with George Harrison in tow, the Plastic Ono Band hurtled off to Abbey Road studios.

When Spector suggested that they needed a huge choir to sing the chorus, John simply asked the ever-dependable Big Mal Evans to go out to the nearest nightclub and bring all the customers back to join in. The record was completed that same night and, with the help of John and Yoko's appearance on "Top of the Pops," it rushed up the charts as fast as the Beatles' "Something" was sliding down.

That the record never went higher than number five may perhaps have been linked with another of John's outrageous acts. A collection of John's erotic lithographs of Yoko, on exhibit at the London Arts Gallery, had been seized by police, who said they were so obscene that they were upsetting passersby. The public merely smiled benignly and put it all down to Yoko, that girl who made the film about bottoms.

The magistrate had been similarly amused and he threw the charge out of court.

Later, a reporter had asked John why so many of his drawings showed him and Yoko in the act of oral sex.

"Because it's fun," he had beamed.

Yoko had become so introspective, so confused in her love for John, that she came to believe that a gang of the Beatles' aides were planning to murder her in order to save the Beatles from disintegration. Though the idea appeared outrageous at first, the more John thought about it, the more plausible it seemed. There were, after all, many, many millions of pounds at stake—much of it slipping away from

George Harrison shortly before the break-up

the hands of highly organized, ruthless businessmen. John's announcement of his intention to quit was common knowledge within the Beatles' circles and it was equally apparent that nothing short of Yoko's departure would persuade him to change his mind. "They all saw me as the most terrifying threat to their cozy little lives," said Yoko.

It would have been naïve to imagine that Yoko's demise would have saved the Beatles. George informed Patti that he would never play with the group again. The years of being submerged beneath the suffocating genius of Paul and John had made him slightly bitter, desperately anxious to fulfill his own potential.

The Beatles' battle to gain control of their music seemed to be ending badly also. When the tussle to gain control of Northern Songs, the company which published the Beatles' music, began, they had all rather enjoyed it. "It's just like playing Monopoly," John had said. But, lately, it seemed to them as though they were playing the game with a gang of cheats. Initially, there had been a fairly straightforward fight between the Beatles and Sir Lew Grade's ATV to gain a majority shareholding. But then in October of 1969 a team of city hustlers and wheeler-dealers had banded together to grab fifteen percent of the remaining shares in anticipation of a quick profit from either the Beatles or ATV. After much bluff and counter-bluff, Sir Lew had won and the Beatles had reluctantly sold out for slightly more than six million dollars.

Paul was bitter about the deal and he began to completely mistrust Allen Klein, whom he'd never signed with in the first place, leaning more and more heavily on John Eastman. Eastman and Klein were now sworn enemies, both constantly bickering and each implying that the other was a cheat and a liar.

It was several months later that Eastman discovered Klein was deliberately holding back Paul's solo album so it would not hit sales of the new Beatles' LP, *Let It Be,* which Spector finally finished and which was due for release in April. After consulting with Paul, Eastman had grabbed the master tape of his album and had threatened to sell it to a rival record company if Capitol Records failed to release it immediately in the U.S. It was then that Ringo made his unsuccessful plea to Paul to postpone the release of his solo album. When the other Beatles realized how vehemently against the suggestion Paul was, they decided instead to postpone *Let It Be* for a month. The arguments and controversy had driven them to the bitter edge.

The Beatles were supposed to release a new single from the new album, but everybody was too busy arguing to decide what it should be. At first someone suggested they put out an old number they had recorded with Brian Jones, "You Know My Name." Then it was a song called "What's the New Mary Jane?" Finally, much to the Beatles' surprise, Paul's song "Let It Be" was released. The decision delighted Paul— the version that had been put out just happened to include Linda plaintively singing harmonies with him. At last, he felt he was even with John for John's "The Ballad of John and Yoko."

That same day that Paul called John about his decision to leave the Beatles, he sent a messenger to every newspaper on Fleet Street with a copy of a carefully self-compiled interview, which he also inserted into the jacket sleeves of his solo album. The "interview" was virtually a declaration of independence."

Q: Why did you decide to make a solo album?

A: Because I got a Studer four-track recording machine at home—practiced on it (playing all instruments)—liked the results and decided to make it into an album.

Q: Were you influenced by John's adventures with the Plastic Ono Band and Ringo's solo LP?

A: Sort of, but not really.

Q: Are all the songs by Paul McCartney alone?

A: Yes, sir.

Q: Will they be so credited: McCartney?

A: It's a bit daft for them to be Lennon-McCartney credited; so McCartney it is.

Q: Did you enjoy working as a solo?

A: Very much, I only had to ask me for a decision, and I agreed with me. Remember, Linda's on it, too; so it's really a double act.

Q: What is Linda's contribution?

A: Strictly speaking, she harmonizes, but, of course, it's more than that because she is a shoulder to lean on, a second opinion, and a photographer of renown. More than all this, she believes in me—constantly. . . .

Q: Are you able to describe the texture or the feel of the theme of the album in a few words?

A: Home, family, love. . . .

Q: Will Linda be heard on all future records?

A: Could be; we love singing together and have plenty of opportunity for practice.

Q: Will Paul and Linda became a John and Yoko?

A: No, they will become Paul and Linda. . . .

Q: What has recording alone taught you?

A: That to make your own decisions about what you do is easy and playing with yourself is difficult but satisfying. . . .

Q: Did you miss the other Beatles and George Martin? Was there a moment, for example, when you thought: "Wish Ringo was here for this break?"

A: No. . . .

Q: Are you planning a new album or single with the Beatles?

A: No. . . .

Q: Is your break with the Beatles temporary or permanent, due to personal differences or musical ones?

A: Personal differences, business differences, musical differences, but most of all because I have a better time with my family. Temporary or permanent? I don't know.

Q: Do you foresee a time when Lennon-McCartney be-
comes an active songwriting partnership again?

A: No. . . .

Q: Have you any plans to set up an independent production
company?

A: McCartney Productions. . . .

It wasn't much but it was enough for Fleet Street. Next
day, a cacophony of headlines screamed to a startled world:
"PAUL QUITS BEATLES."

John was mortified. Paul was telling the world that he had
decided to end the Beatles, when John felt that he had
started the group and that it was for him to end it.

A few days later, he snarled to reporters: "It's John,
George, and Ringo as individuals. We're not even communicating with or making plans about Paul. . . ."

The break-up was complete. The Beatles were the Beatles
no more.

WHERE DO WE GO
FROM HERE

6

TEARS TRICKLED DOWN John's face: "Oh, Christ, fucking Christ. . . ." he sobbed. All the suppressed agony he'd stored inside himself was seeking release, the pain inflicted by the father who abandoned him, the mother who died just as he had begun to win her love, the broken marriage, the broken career, the phoniness. Slowly, he let out a piercing, chilling scream, like a stag when the hounds have it by the throat.

Neither John nor Yoko had been prepared for the shock they were to feel when the longed-for break-up of the Beatles finally became reality. Instead of the long-anticipated sense of freedom, there was loss; instead of triumph, there was despondency. They secreted themselves at Tittenhurst Park, living only in the bedroom or the kitchen, refusing to speak to anyone except through Anthony Fawcett, their personal assistant, or Valerie, their housekeeper. Sometimes they would spend whole days lying in bed watching horse-racing, "Andy Pandy," "Panorama," and everything else that came up on the ceaselessly flickering screen.

Frequently, they would fight one another with their claws out. More and more, John was cutting himself off just as he had done when he couldn't cope as a little boy living with his Auntie Mimi or, later, when he was married to Cynthia. He smoked too much dope, refused even to talk to the builders who were hard at work on the gargantuan task of restoring their little-used mansion. Deep inside, it seemed, he missed the Beatles. There were occasional bright spots twinkling amidst the gloom—like the day of Yoko's thirty-seventh birthday when he took her to stay at the Inn on the Park Hotel in London, and ordered the whole of the vast suite to be filled with red roses as a surprise. But, mostly, their relationship was falling apart, just as surely as his marriage to Cynthia had fallen apart. The storms had even battered Yoko's oaken strength so that his cruel words could reduce her to paroxysms of weeping.

It was all so different from the first time they had made love together, back in 1968. It had taken place one evening while Cynthia was in Greece. John, after puzzling for hours over the letters Yoko had been sending him, telephoned her to ask if she would like to come over. When she arrived, she was as tense and excited as he was and, at first, their conversation was stilted and giggly. John had never been particularly skilled at small talk—he had done nothing but work in the studio and watch TV for weeks, and very rapidly they ran out of things to say.

"Do you want to hear some of the things I've been playing around at in my studio?" he asked awkwardly. And so they had gone upstairs together. John had played her some silly comedy tapes and when she collapsed into fits of sweet, childish giggles, he felt confident enough to play her some of his strange, hypnotic electronic music—pieces too outlandish for the Beatles even to consider.

When the tape was over, they rolled a couple of joints and sat down to play at making a record together. John rattled out some pub piano, Yoko wailed, and they tried burping simultaneously onto the tape. All in all it was every bit as silly as John's games with his mother, Julia, had been.

Later, at dawn, they crawled exhausted to the bedroom and made love with a passion John had never known with any other woman. Yoko, who had been married twice before, made love with a physical power and a vivid imagination which left John literally dizzy. After the gentle serenity of his life with Cyn, he felt as though he had been hurled from a gentle park lake to the midst of a Pacific typhoon. He woke later the next evening to feel her lying beside him, softly stroking his hair. He knew his life would never be the same again.

From that very first night, Yoko had penetrated deep into John's being; he loved her with the all-consuming passion of a warrior for his country or a zealot for his god.

"I don't know how it happened," he said later. "I just realized that she knew everything I knew, and more probably, and that it was coming out of a woman's head. It just sort of bowled me over. It was like finding gold or something, to find somebody that you could go and get pissed with, and have exactly the same relationship as any mate in Liverpool you ever had. But you could go to bed with it, and it could stroke your head when you felt tired, or sick or depressed. It could also be mother. As she was talking to me I would get high, and the discussion would get to such a level that I would be going higher and higher. When she'd leave, I'd go back to this sort of suburbia. Then I'd meet her again and my head would go open like I was on an acid trip."

But now, gradually, following the break-up of the Beatles, they had become undone. They were in urgent need of treatment, and yet neither of them seemed to have sufficient strength to call out for help.

One day a friend who was traveling through the States on business mailed them a copy of a newly published book by Dr. Arthur Janov entitled *The Primal Scream*. Taking Freud as his starting point, Janov, who is a celebrated American psychiatrist, evolved the theory that all neurosis stems from a lack of parental love, a lack of fulfillment of basic needs when a person is a small child. A multitude of small incidents begin the process, culminating in what Janov calls the "major primal scene," which usually occurs when the child is between five and seven years old. At that age, the child is mature enough to see some kind of significance in all the small, unsettling incidents which have worried him in the past; at that point, it only takes one minor trauma to crystallize the child's attitude and to push him or her firmly on the path toward neurosis. The way to help the individual to come to terms with his neurosis, says Janov, is to persuade him to return to and then to cease repressing these unpleasant experiences. Janov encourages the patient to scream belatedly at his absent parents, in order to exorcise the ghosts that are haunting him.

John and Yoko fell on the book like starving people on charity soup. To them it seemed to offer a glimmer of hope, like sun peeping through a chink in a black and gloomy sky. But John was cautious: acid had seemed to offer salvation at one time, but it had only left him more confused than he was before. The Maharishi, too, had proved a false prophet. But, after days of argument, the two of them decided they had little to lose and much to gain. They waited until it was late afternoon at Ascot (early morning in Los Angeles) and telephoned Dr. Janov at his Primal Institute. He sounded confident, relaxed, enormously patient, not at all taken aback by this cry for help from two of the most famous entertainers in the world. Quietly, he spoke to each of them, asking them why they felt they would benefit from primal therapy. Then he asked them both to write him long letters telling him about their childhoods, their problems, and what they were hoping to achieve.

Excited at the thought of actually moving forward, of doing something positive at last, they had both written and mailed their letters that night.

John's childhood, as retold in his letter, was often a painful one. He had been born to Fred and Julia Lennon in 1940 amidst a blizzard of Hitler's bombs. Fred was off at sea somewhere, waiting on cruise ships, and the marriage was virtually over before John arrived. When, eventually, Julia met a new man, John was sent off to live with her sister, Mimi. Then, when he was five and the war was over, John's father had turned up again and taken him off to live in

Blackpool. It appeared as though the two of them were to stay together forever, but a few weeks later Julia turned up on the doorstep to say she wanted him back. John's father told the bewildered boy he could do whatever he liked, and he found himself cruelly forced to choose between his parents. At first, he decided he would stay with his father, but when Julia walked away, John suddenly leaped up and ran down the street after her, crying that he wanted to be with them both. John had become a millionaire Beatle before he saw his father again.

He was brought up by his Auntie Mimi and Uncle George. Whenever he had tried to talk with them about his parents, they had avoided his questions, and he found himself taking refuge in a world of fantasy, dreaming, writing stories. He had become confused and just a little unhappy. There were so many half-remembered things—strange, frightening incidents which he couldn't properly explain to himself.

When John was twelve, Uncle George died. But, by that time, the most important person in John's life was his mother. Though she was in her early thirties, Julia reveled in skylarking like a naughty teen-ager with John and his friends: she told him jokes, laughed at the teachers, and he grew to love her soft voice and tinkling laugh more than anything he knew. She taught him to play banjo, which he practiced until his fingers bled, just to please her. She bought him a guitar and showed him how to pick out chords. When he said he wanted to form a group, she encouraged him in that as well. She seemed more like a wonderful best friend than a mother.

When John was seventeen, Julia came to visit him at Mimi's house, where he still lived. She was waiting at the bus stop to go home when a drunk off-duty policeman ran her down and killed her.

"That was the second big trauma for me," John related. "I lost her twice: when I was five and I moved in with my auntie, and when she physically died. That made me more bitter; the chip I had on my shoulder I had as a youth got really big then. I was just reestablishing the relationship with her and she was killed.

"The copper came to the door to tell us about the accident. It was just like it's supposed to be, the way it is in the films. Asking if I was her son and all that. Then he told us, and we both went white. It was the worst thing that ever happened to me. I thought: 'I've no responsibilities to anyone now.'"

He had rampaged around Liverpool like a wounded buffalo—drinking, fighting, screwing, creating mayhem at every turn.

Yoko's letter was quite a bit different. Yoko had been born in 1933 to a wealthy Tokyo banker, who was a frustrated classical pianist, and a socialite mother, who was a frustrated artist. Both envisioned Yoko as a means of vicariously fulfilling their dreams.

Yoko was seven when World War Two began. Her parents left Yoko to the care of servants in their safe, remote country house. But, within months, the servants deserted their charge, leaving her to scrounge and scrabble for food as best she could until her parents returned.

Yoko was in her mid-teens when her father was appointed as Japan's representative to the United Nations, and the family moved to the elegant New York suburb of Scarsdale—by curious coincidence, only a few streets away from Linda Eastman's family.

Yoko went to the prim Sarah Lawrence College, where she studied art and philosophy. When she was twenty-six, she married an impecunious Japanese pianist named Toci Ichianagi. They lived in Greenwich Village but rapidly drifted apart as she became increasingly engrossed in Dada and the art of Andy Warhol.

Art to Yoko at that time meant watching a sheet of paper burn or rolling her body along the keyboard of a piano. Misery at the breakdown of her marriage, coupled with the refusal of the world to take her work seriously, drove Yoko to a deep depression which culminated in her admission to a psychiatric hospital after a suicide attempt in Tokyo. It was while she was in the hospital that her old friend, Tony Cox, had come to visit her, had asked her to marry him, and, very soon afterwards, Kyoko was born.

Yoko and Tony had been living together in London when she had fallen in love with John.

In their letters, John and Yoko asked whether Janov would come to England to help them. They did not feel it would be possible for them to travel to California without their treatment becoming a circus for the world's press. The psychiatrist agreed to their request and he issued them with a lengthy list of instructions in preparation for their treatment: they were to immediately stop smoking, drinking alcohol, and taking any drugs whatsoever—even aspirin. Then, twenty-four hours before his arrival, they were each to go to separate bedrooms, where they were to wait for him without watching television, listening to the radio, reading, or speaking to anyone—even on the telephone. To John and Yoko, this was the most difficult request of all: they had been apart only very infrequently since they had moved in together early in 1968.

Janov arrived, charmed Anthony and Valerie, then proceeded straight to John's bedroom. Closing the curtains so the room was in semidarkness, he asked John to lay spread-eagled on his back, defenseless, then he began gently to ask him about his tensions, his problems, and his childhood.

Gently, Janov began to urge him to concentrate more and more on the unhappiness of his childhood: "Feel that, stay with it," he encouraged each time John began to open up.

The session went on for almost two hours. Then, after a short break, Dr. Janov went on to repeat the gentle coaxing and relaxing process with Yoko.

This part of the treatment, said Dr. Janov, was called the pre-primal. Essentially, it consisted of breaking down all their reserves, persuading them to totally open up to themselves.

After a week, he advised them to stay in separate hotel suites in order to completely isolate themselves from everything and everyone. John, who now looked fragile and exhausted, moved into the Inn on the Park while Yoko took a suite in another hotel a few blocks away. Each day, Janov came to see them, to talk with them for three hours or more until they began, increasingly, to understand their hang-ups.

"I was never really wanted when I was a child," John realized. "The only reason I am a star is because of my repressions. The only reason I went for that goal is that I wanted to say: 'Now, Mummy, will you love me?'"

His Aunt Mimi had always told him his parents had fallen out of love, he remembered. No matter how much he had asked she would never tell him why he could not live with them, what had happened to them. Once, he remembered, his mother had fallen on her way to visit him when he was small, arriving with torn stockings and blood on her face. He hid until she had gone away. He didn't want anyone to see the misery her hurt had caused him. Years later, just when it seemed he had at last won her love, she had been killed. John steeled himself just as he had as a small boy, and had shown no emotion.

After Julia's death, she had been replaced in John's affection by a student he met at art school named Stuart Sutcliffe. Stu was a brilliant painter, but he had never played a musical instrument in his life. John wanted him in the Beatles, however, so Stu had been prevailed upon to purchase a bass guitar. He had looked wonderful with his gaunt cheekbones and Marlon Brando shades but he had played so badly that he had spent most of his time with his back to the group's audiences in the hope that they wouldn't realize he only knew two chords.

In 1961, Stuart had left the Beatles to marry a beautiful girl he had met in Hamburg and to enroll at art college there. But the empathy and love which he and John felt for one another remained undimmed. Often John would write him letters twenty pages or more long: Stu, it seemed, was the only person in the world who understood him now that Julia was dead. So while John remained a tough guy with most people, once even mugging a German sailor for his money—it was only to Stu that he showed his soft vulnerability.

Stu had died of a brain disease in the spring of 1962. John painfully suppressed his feelings of loss. This time, scarcely a trace of a frown had crossed John's face. Later, by the time of Brian Epstein's death, John seemed to have become emotionally untouchable.

Gently, Janov coaxed John to cry all the tears he had never cried—for his mother, for Stu, for himself. It was a cathartic experience and, after two weeks of crying, screaming, and solitude in their hotel suites, John and Yoko had felt somehow cleansed, eager to continue. When Dr. Janov told them he wanted them both to travel to Los Angeles with him, they had ordered their aides to lock up Tittenhurst Park, to close down their office at Apple, and to arrange for them to stay with their friend, Phil Spector, who lived close to the Primal Institute. They spent two half-days a week in painful group therapy at the Institute for four months. Most of the sessions culminated with both of them screaming and sobbing, but gradually they were coming to terms with their lives, learning to decide what they wanted.

Then, quite suddenly, they decided that they did not wish to continue the therapy, and they hopped on a plane to Heathrow.

"Janov showed me how to feel my own fear and pain," John told a journalist soon afterwards. "Therefore, I can handle it better than I could before, that's all. I'm just the same, only there's a channel. It doesn't just remain in me, it goes round and out. I can move a little easier. I still think that Janov's therapy is great, you know, but I don't want to make it into a big Maharishi thing. If people know what I've been through there, and if they want to find out, they can find out, otherwise it turns into that again.

"I don't think anything else would work on me. But then, of course, I'm not through with it; it's a process that is going on. We primal almost daily. You see, I don't want to get this big primal thing going because it's so embarrassing. The thing in a nutshell: primal therapy allowed us to feel feelings continually, and those feelings usually make you cry. That's all. I was blocking the feelings, and when the feelings come through, you cry. It's as simple as that, really."

7

ALL THE PUBLICITY Paul had received from announcing his decision to quit the Beatles had blown up in his face. The critics were waiting with machetes raised when his solo album finally reached the shops on April 17. Paul had deliberately recorded the album simply and unpretentiously on very basic equipment in order to recapture the rawness which he felt was missing from later Beatle albums. But his intention was entirely misunderstood, with the result that the record into which he had poured so much love and care was condemned as only amateurish and banal.

For a short time, Paul retreated to his High Park Farm in Scotland. High Park Farm floated like a raft in the sea of lush purple heather and tangled green bracken that rises over the lonely Mull of Kintyre. The farmhouse is an austere, bleak place whose ravaged granite walls and ugly corrugated iron roof speak of winters buried beneath snow and springs of lashing, driving rain blowing in from the Atlantic Ocean. The house, with its one hundred and eighty acres of barren land, hides like a cowering animal at the end of a narrow, little-used lane five miles from the tiny town of Machrihanish in Scotland.

Paul had bought the farm when he was still dating Jane Asher as a place where they could go when he wanted to ride his horses, grow his vegetables, and stop being a Beatle. They had been happy there, walking in the fields and shopping in the local shops without any of the headaches of fans sitting on the doorstep or people screaming for autographs. Linda, too, had fallen in love with High Park when he took her there shortly before their wedding. She had dashed around with her Nikon, filled with enthusiasm for the desolate, rejuvenating beauty of the place. "The light in Scotland is the best light in the world for me," she said later. "The incredible beauty in old rocks and moss. The sky, the changes in the weather. It's good."

By contrast to Paul's solo album, the ill-starred Beatles' *Let It Be* was hailed as a triumph and sold nearly five million copies around the world in its first week of release.

The success of *Let It Be* grated particularly on Paul because one of Paul's songs on the album, "The Long and Winding Road," had been savagely rearranged by Phil Spector. Paul had pleaded with Klein for the song to be changed before the record was released, but his entreaties were flatly ignored.

Paul had also tried to prevent Klein bringing out the film of *Let It Be* because he appeared to feel it would show him in such a bad light that he would become even more unpopular with the fans. He and Lee Eastman attempted to argue that the movie had been made on 16mm film and that it would therefore be unsuitable for general release. Klein merely chuckled when he heard the complaint. George, too, seemed to hope the film would end up in the incinerator. He had cringed with humiliation when he had seen Paul bullying him in the rough version of the movie, even telling him how to play guitar, as though he were an incompetent session musician and Paul a musical wizard. At one point, in an effort to assert himself, George—looking like a recalcitrant student cheeking a teacher—had been filmed mumbling awkwardly to Paul: "Look, I'll play whatever you want—I'll play if you want me to play, I won't play if you don't want me to play—but just shut up with all this."

George knew that all the musicians whose approbation he craved would have a good laugh over that one.

Regardless of everyone's feelings, *Let It Be* opened in New York, London, and Liverpool in May and played to packed houses.

Paul didn't want to speak to any of the others now. He felt humiliated, felt (quite rightly) that they would be pleased and amused by the hostile reaction to McCartney. In a symbolic rejection of everything which Apple had represented, he rented a little office up four flights of stairs in Soho with worn linoleum on the floor and just a few battered desks and broken filing cabinets for furniture. He had asked a friend, writer Shelley Turner, to help run things for him until he managed to organize a permanent staff and she had readily agreed.

His first, slightly confused, move toward becoming a businessman came when he purchased the rights to make an animated film about the celebrated cartoon character "Rupert the Bear"—he and the other Beatles had always seen something faintly "trippy" about Rupert's surreal life-style.

While John and Paul wallowed ever deeper in the mire of self-pity and melancholy, George had skipped effortlessly past them to produce an album which was vastly superior to anything his erstwhile leaders had managed to achieve on their own.

Previously, while the Beatles were still together, he had made two attempts at solo projects—*Wonderwall Music* and *Electronic Sound*—and both had proved to be only self-indulgent and silly.

But after the break-up, armed with the confidence of his hit Beatles' single, "Something," George suddenly found himself outstripping his mentors.

"Once the last Beatles' album was finished, I was raring to go," he recalled later. "I'd got so much music inside me that I was musically constipated."

He had persuaded Bob Dylan to help him on a new album—something John Lennon had failed to achieve a year previously when Dylan had refused to play on "Cold Turkey." And then he had called on almost every famous musician he knew to help to turn the album into a blockbuster. Eric Clapton, Klaus Voorman, Alan White, Billy Preston, Ginger Baker, Gary Brooker, and even Ringo, were all hauled in to add punch.

Cramming this huge array of talent onto a single LP proved impossible, of course. The record, entitled *All Things Must Pass*, stretched to a triple album, forcing it to be sold for a most unaltruistic ten dollars.

One track immediately leaped out at all who heard it. The song was called "My Sweet Lord" and it was about George's desire to understand and become one with his Lord, sung to a girl chorus repeating "Hare Krishna" in the background. The song seemed as if it were advertising a new kind of chocolate bar. Anything less spiritual would have been hard to imagine.

But it was the instant commercial appeal of the song which surprised almost everyone who heard it. Unfortunately for George, the song bore an uncanny similarity to an old hit by the Chiffons called "He's So Fine." This was later to cause George a great deal of legal difficulty.

"He must have known, you know," John Lennon was to say later. "He's smarter than that. He could have changed a couple of bars in that song and nobody could ever have touched him, but he just let it go. Maybe he thought God would just sort of let him off."

Certainly the Almighty seemed to be on George's side when the record was released. "My Sweet Lord" instantly became the first record by any of the ex-Beatles to make number one on the charts, and *All Things Must Pass* became one of the best-selling albums of all time, despite its high price.

After all the unkind things which had been said about *Sentimental Journey,* Ringo drifted out to Nashville, where he recruited the best session men he could find and cut an LP of country and western songs called *Beaucoups of Blues.* It wasn't a record to set the world on fire but it was less embarrassing than his previous effort.

He still lived in a mock-Tudor house like John's, just around the corner from John in Weybridge. Both John's and Ringo's houses had been selected for them by their accountants in the days when they had been too busy singing to worry about trivial things like house-hunting.

Ringo and Allen Klein on the set of Blind Man, *released in 1971.*

Ringo's place was called Sunny Heights. He had plenty to occupy him there—supervising the team of landscape gardeners, watching home movies in his private screening room, or playing with Zak and Jason or his youngest child.

His married life was still going well. Maureen, being a northern lass, had always known her place in Ringo's life: in the home. He had married her when she was a pretty, dark-haired eighteen-year-old hairdresser from Liverpool at Caxton Hall on February 11, 1965. Maureen had been his girlfriend before he had even thought about joining the Beatles, so he knew that she loved him for himself and that she wasn't just another besotted fan.

In the days of the Beatles, if Ringo had to record late, she would always make sure a steaming hot stew or a huge plate of roast beef and Yorkshire pudding was waiting for him when he got home—even if it was five in the morning. Then, when he woke up next afternoon, she would bring him his breakfast in bed. They had loved one another deeply then, and they loved one another now.

With all the Beatles gone their separate ways, floundering to find themselves in their new careers, Apple had become an anachronism, an awkward reminder of a dead idealism. The idealistic intentions behind Apple had, of course, been dead for a long time. The boutique, the Fool, had been an unmitigated disaster. But the boutique was merely the tip of the iceberg. Accounts for the first few months of the company's existence—before things really went crazy—showed that three cars had been purchased by the company, but nobody had been quite sure who they had been bought for or where they had gone. Numerous advances had also to be written off, including one of $2,000 to Magic Alex (that was rumored to have been for yet another car) and one of $4,000 to another employee.

The Beatles had discovered that they could no longer trust anyone. They had endeavored to surround themselves with their old friends from Liverpool. Neil Aspinall, their original road manager, had been suddenly thrust into the role of managing director. Mal Evans was made a senior executive, as were several other lovely people with minimal business experience. That didn't really matter, the Beatles had said, because they were in the business of creativity, not making money. As long as Apple covered its costs, that was all that mattered. In fact, so sordid did they find money that they hadn't even wanted their accounts department at Savile Row. That should be far away, hidden under a dark stone somewhere, where it belonged.

Apple became the biggest, wildest, freakiest party in town. Anyone working in the record industry or for a newspaper, radio, or television station had been welcome to drop in any time to drink themselves silly or to smoke a little grass. There had been poetry readings, light shows, and inventors entertaining people all day long. The machine had taken on a life of its own.

The Beatles had strolled in and out countermanding one another's orders, no longer communicating, desperately trying to prove to themselves and to the world-at-large that they were individual people with their own thoughts and attitudes, not merely single components of the Fab Four. Somehow most of the staff at Apple had found it all difficult to comprehend—even they had believed in the myth of the Beatles. Neil and Mal understood, though. Mal, particularly, had long been nonplussed by the way in which the world saw the Beatles as demigods.

"They're ordinary blokes and they can be really nasty bastards when someone gets their backs up," he once confided. "Yet people don't want to believe, somehow, that they are human—that they can be vicious and petty and mean."

Inevitably, the house of cards had to tumble. "Apple was full of hustlers and spongers," John told *Rolling Stone* later.

"The staff came and went as they pleased and were lavish with money and hospitality. We have since discovered that at around that time two of Apple's cars had completely disappeared and also that we owned a house which no one can remember buying.

"People were robbing us and living on us to the tune of . . . eighteen or twenty thousand pounds a week was rolling out of Apple and nobody was doing anything about it. All our buddies that worked for us for fifty years were just living and drinking and eating like fucking Rome, and I suddenly realized it and said we're losing money at such a rate that we would have been broke, really broke. We didn't have anything in the bank, really, none of us did. Paul and I could probably have floated, but we were sinking fast. It was just hell, and it had to stop."

It took the Beatles a little too long to learn that even beautiful people with hair over their shoulders and floral shirts could be thieves. Electric typewriters, television sets, hi-fi systems, cases of wine, and gold records were pillaged daily. Anyone with sufficient nerve to walk in off the street and help themselves could probably count on taking their booty away through the front door, straight past the super-cool security man. Things had to go out of the front door because there wasn't even a back door.

One of the most enterprising rackets had been operated by the mail carriers, who would arrive with sacks full of mail—much of which was destined never to be opened in the chaos—and then leave with their sacks filled with lead from the Apple roof.

Somehow helping oneself to things from Apple didn't feel like theft, say people who used to work there. The Beatles were richer than Croesus and, like working-class people who had just won an undeserved fortune in a football pool, they seemed to have a guilty compulsion to splash their fortune around among their old friends.

Certainly, the Beatles themselves did nothing to encourage abstemiousness: although they had a kitchen lavishly stocked with the finest foods from Fortnum & Mason, John had once flown into a rage when Yoko asked for caviar only to find that none had been purchased. "If you know she is coming, there should always be some caviar for her," he had fumed.

Thereafter, a messenger was dispatched to Fortnum's to buy an eighty dollar jar of caviar each time there seemed to be a possibility that Miss Ono would be paying a state visit. Often, she would only be in the mood for brown rice with steamed vegetables or she simply wouldn't turn up, and so the caviar would be taken home by anyone who wanted it. John had also developed a taste for a rare type of vodka which could only be purchased through an exotic Knightsbridge restaurant at three times the normal price for vodka. The chosen brand had been the only one served to guests at Apple, of course.

There had been occasional triumphs, also—not with films or shops or books, about which the Beatles knew very little, of course. But with music, about which they knew almost everything. Jane Asher's bespectacled and brilliant brother, Peter Asher, who had once been half of the successful singing duo Peter and Gordon, had been appointed head of A & R. And, since he was very bright, he was able to help Mary Hopkin, a little-known seventeen-year-old blonde girl from Wales, to achieve nationwide fame and fortune with a Paul McCartney song called "Those Were the Days." Bad-finger also proved successful, as did James Taylor.

On the whole, however, Apple had been a catastrophe. When Allen Klein at last had a chance to sink his teeth into Apple in the Sixties, the result was not so much a spring cleaning as a purge. Ron Kass, the tanned, elegant head of Apple's record division, had been the first to feel Klein's steel-tipped boot. There had soon followed Alistair Taylor, the company's office manager; Brian Lewis, their business consultant; Dennis O'Dell, their head of films; Peter Asher, their

A & R man; and several secretaries and minor aides. After the break-up, the last few stragglers from "the world's longest cocktail party" were thrown out onto Savile Row and Apple became simply the Beatles' accounts department, just as Allen Klein had always intended it should.

8

SAVAGELY JOHN TORE at his guitar, screaming wildly to his lost mother: " . . . you had me but I never had you." Tears streamed down his face, losing themselves in his billowing beard. Behind him, Ringo looked woefully at his drums, feeling awkward, pretending not to notice. John had always seemed so strong in the early days that even Ringo had feared his cruel tongue. Now a very different John spent the greater part of every recording session sobbing: for his lost mother, for women, for himself.

John and Yoko had returned to their recording studio, which had been built at Tittenhurst Park in their absence, bubbling over with enthusiasm, eager to record all the songs they had written about their group therapy session in California. He had phoned Ringo, who had been eager to join in since he was becoming bored with just sitting around the house with Maureen and their three children. And then he had called Klaus Voorman, an old friend who had played with the Beatles on-and-off since their earliest days in Hamburg.

He had chosen the two of them because he felt easy with them, they had seen him pilled and drunk, known him when he used to punch noses instead of punching for peace. Above all, he didn't feel they would inhibit him in the music he wanted to create. The resultant album, *John Lennon/Plastic*

Ono Band, was stark, hideous, and compelling. It was, most thoughtful critics agreed, not a pop record at all but a serious work of art comparable more to an agonized Van Gogh self-portrait than to the lively, jolly dross of the hit parade. Songs with titles like "My Mummy's Dead" didn't fit into the commercial structure of the music business. John sang of his loneliness in "Working-Class Hero." And finally, perhaps most telling of all, he spelled out the things he didn't believe in anymore: the Bible (as a teen-ager he had so believed that he had been confirmed at his local church in Liverpool), Magic Alex (Magic Alex had betrayed his trust), the *I Ching* (he had never made a serious decision at Apple without consulting it). He concluded his bitter litany, screaming, "I don't believe in Beatles . . ." and "the dream is over. . . ."

Just as the Beatles had changed, so had the world. In Britain Harold Wilson's "Walter Mitty" government gave way to the "Don Quixote" administration of Edward Heath. New words began to enter the language—words like ecology, conservation, and preservation—gradually superseding the old touchstones like progress, liberation, and renewal.

The Beatles' joyous, optimistic music of the early days had only been an exaggerated reflection of an age gone by. Many sensed that the Seventies to come would be in many ways the most important decade since the industrial revolution. A turning point had been reached: for the first time, the previously unquestionable concept of the ceaseless improvement of man's condition and comfort by means of high technology were being reexamined, and ideas which had previously been accepted as gospel were being questioned anew. John was to remain as much a symbol (albeit sadder and less acceptable) of the Seventies as he had of the Sixties.

Paul gulped down another large Scotch, softened with the tiniest slug of Coke, lit a fresh cigarette from the one already in his nicotine-stained fingers, and turned to Lee Eastman:

"So what can I do to stop Klein being my manager?" he asked.

"That's easy," said Eastman. "Sue him."

"OK, let's do it. Great, I don't care."

"Yes, but it's not quite that simple," said the lawyer. "To get at him, you'll have to sue Apple and, as John, George, and Ringo are your fellow directors, that will mean suing them as well."

"Well, that's out of the question," said Paul. "We'll have to work something else out."

Eastman had suggested that Paul should simply try asking the other three to let him go. There was, however, one small drawback: each time he tried to phone any of them, they were inclined to simply tell him to go away and stop bothering them. The threats to Ringo, and the egocentric way in which Paul had announced the break-up still rankled.

Paul tried writing to John, telling him they were all caught in the same trap but that they could all let one another out of it. John responded by sending him a cartoon of himself and Yoko with a balloon coming from his own mouth which read: "How and why?"

"How?" replied Paul. "By all signing a piece of paper agreeing to dissolve the Apple partnership. Why? Because we don't have a partnership anymore."

A few days later, a postcard arrived in Paul's letter-box on Cavendish Avenue bearing the cryptic message: "Get well soon. Get the other signatures and I will think about it."

A few weeks later, the Inland Revenue tossed a squib into the smoldering bonfire in the shape of a writ against the Beatles for not filling in their tax forms.

Paul phoned George but was icily told that breaking up the partnership now would cost hundreds of thousands of pounds because of their delicate tax situation. That's what Klein had told George, anyway.

In desperation, Paul had talked with Linda's brother, John Eastman, about the problem. "You've got no choice," he was advised. "Either you sue him and the others or you are stuck with him as your manager for the next six years. Klein is a bullshitter and a shark and he thinks you are just chicken-shit. You've got to get rid of him."

There had, of course, been furious rows between Klein and Lee Eastman in the last days of the Beatles. Once, in front of all the Beatles, Eastman had lost his temper with Klein and started shouting at him until all of them except Paul told Eastman to shut up, that Klein was in the right. Klein's one masterstroke had been the cajoling of EMI to agree to up the Beatles' royalty from ten percent to twenty-five percent. That was a deal even Paul had been happy to sign. But Klein had lost an attempt to gain control of the Beatles' management company, NEMS, as well as the Beatles' music publishers, Northern Songs. Paul had grown to mistrust Klein, and had gradually found himself siding with Lee Eastman against Klein and the others. The last straw had been Klein's attempt to hold up the release of Paul's solo album.

By Christmas, Paul had almost made up his mind to sue Klein, but as he walked around his farm with John Eastman, he asked plaintively: "And you are absolutely certain there is nothing I can do except to sue the others . . . it's going to be very messy."

"Very. . . ."

A week later, Paul issued a writ asking for the partnership to be wound up and a receiver appointed to deal with their money. He said the Beatles no longer performed together and that, therefore, the purpose of their partnership had gone, that he had never received audited accounts of their financial position, and that the appointment of Klein was in breach of the original partnership deal.

Characteristically, John responded by giving an extraor-dinarily candid interview to *Rolling Stone*, in which he compared Paul with Engelbert Humperdinck and com-mented: "After Brian died, we collapsed. Paul took over and supposedly led us. But what is leading us when we went

Brian Epstein, the Beatles' manager

round in circles? We broke up then. That was the disintegration."

Even when Brian was alive, though, there were myriad problems behind the scenes. Brian Epstein had been in love with John since the day he first saw the Beatles sweating and screaming beneath the dripping walls of the Cavern Club in Liverpool. Brian was a homosexual with a penchant for "rough trade"—cruel, young boys. He loved John's combination of prettiness and wickedness, his deep sensitivity and his brutality; he got off on his extravagant cowboy boots; his clinging, black leather suits; his soft, floppy hair. And John,

despite his macho persona, seemed to actively encourage
Brian's camp flirtations. Brian would frequently put his arm
around John's shoulders or his hand on his knee. "There was
a closeness between us," John said later. "Looking back, I
suppose he fancied me and I liked all the attention he was
giving me."

Shortly after Cynthia had given birth to John's son, Julian,
John told Cynthia that he and Brian Epstein were going on
vacation together. She knew Brian was homosexual, sensed
as a woman that he had developed a passion for John and she
was worried. "It hit me like a bolt out of the blue when John
said they were going off to Spain," she said. "I really didn't
take it in properly at first but when it sank in I suppressed my
true feelings and aquiesced."

John always denied that he and Brian went to bed together
during the spring holiday in Spain: "But we did have a pretty
intense relationship," he said. The pair of them would sit
together in pavement cafés watching the boys go by, joking
and flirting together. As well as being flattered by the
attention, John was intrigued by Brian's passion for literature, his love for Sibelius.

While in Spain, they met up briefly with the Shadows, who
remarked later on the obvious closeness between the two
men.

Later, when John and Brian returned to England, the other
Beatles were surly, offhanded, refusing to believe they had
not had an affair.

When John's old friend, Bob Wooler—who had been the
disc jockey at the Cavern—began to tease him about his
"romance," John went berserk and beat him so savagely that
he needed hospital treatment and later began a legal action
against him. The case was hastily hushed up and Wooler was
paid off with four hundred dollars in cash. It was the last real
fight John ever had.

Though Paul hadn't said anything, it was obvious to those
around the band that he resented the way Epstein had
muscled his way into John's affections.

But the problems under Brian's reign had gone beyond his particularly close relationship with John. Inevitably, Brian had made many financial blunders—some of which seem hard to believe now that rock 'n' roll has become a slick, multibillion-dollar worldwide industry. Perhaps his worst mistake came when hundreds of traders began cashing in on the Beatles' success by manufacturing millions of dollars worth of Beatles memorabilia. Third-rate plastic toys, hideous wigs, hot water bottles: it seemed anything would sell if it carried the magical Beatles insignia.

Brian was so busy organizing concerts and records that he had asked his solicitor, David Jacobs, to take the problem off his shoulders. Jacobs decided to hand the whole Beatles' merchandising operation over to a company which would be capable of producing goods of a quality high enough not to besmirch the Beatles' reputation. This company would also be able to stamp out all the manufacturers of phony souvenirs.

The man Jacobs had wanted to head this company was an elegant young socialite named Nicky Byrne. Byrne's wife, Kiki, had just designed a line of leather skiwear in partnership with Lord Snowdon—a line which had been colorfully sported on the slopes by Princess Margaret.

He was elegant, articulate, well-connected, and, in every way, perfect for the job, Jacobs decided.

Byrne had said he would be happy to produce Beatles' goods and to track down the pirates. He would, he offered magnanimously, pay the Beatles ten percent of all the company earned.

Astonishingly, both Epstein and Jacobs agreed to the deal, effectively throwing away ninety percent of the millions upon millions of dollars that were to be earned by Beatles' products. Byrne gleefully set up a European marketing company called Stramsact and a United States equivalent called Seltaeb—Beatles spelled backwards. It was estimated that in 1964 the American company alone earned $50 million.

The vast sums of money involved generated enormous pressures. American big business desperately wanted to buy Seltaeb out. Brian tried to undermine the company when he realized the multibillion-dollar scale of his mistake, finally suing them for alleged nonpayment of merchandising royalties. Then Byrne's partners in the companies also became uneasy about his antics and they, too, instructed their lawyers to take action against him.

The whole mess dragged through the courts for nearly three years, earning in the process many formidable enemies for both Brian Epstein and David Jacobs. Though it is difficult to estimate just how much that one blunder cost the Beatles themselves, one top record company executive believes the figure could well be as high as $100 million.

But neither Brian nor the band had time to think of such things then. They seemed to be living in a disorienting whirl of nonstop concerts. Brian had other concerns on his mind as well. He was deeply involved in a world of male prostitutes and late-night pickups—a dangerous game. The boys knew exactly who he was and most of them were not above a little blackmail—homosexuality then was not regarded in the enlightened way it is today: publicity about Brian's preferences would have had serious repercussions for the Beatles' business empire. Brian didn't even want the Beatles to know how he spent his nights and so he became increasingly secretive, returning to his London house on Chapel Street, Belgravia, at dawn and gulping down handfuls of powerful barbiturate sleeping tablets to help obliterate the memories of the night before.

The reality of John's wishful memories of a strongly united and together Beatles was as ephemeral as the Beatles' belief that they could separate themselves from the rest of humanity, a race unto themselves—an impossibility that was best underscored in the Greek island fiasco.

It was, of course, to Brian Epstein that the Beatles turned when the notion came into their heads.

"You want to what?" Brian Epstein had asked Paul.

"That's right, we want to buy our own island off Greece like the one Aristotle Onassis has," said Paul, looking at Brian superciliously. "We want to go somewhere we can escape, somewhere no one can get at us."

Brian had felt uncomfortable. There was something about Paul—the inner ruthlessness, the thinly veiled contempt in his eyes—that had always made Brian feel uneasy, right from the Liverpool days when he had first become their manager. John he loved, George and Ringo were malleable—but Paul frightened him.

Nevertheless, Brian would happily have chopped his thumb off if he believed it was what the Beatles truly wanted and so he had hastily begun negotiations to buy the island for them. Agreeing to the purchase took only a few days, but then had come the problem of arranging for money to be taken out of Britain, for stringent controls then limited the amount of cash which could leave the country. Nevertheless, such was the sway of the Beatles that members of Parliament and Treasury officials agreed to grant them special dispensation. It was felt that they had brought so much into the country that they earned the right to their refuge.

"It will be amazing," John had enthused. "We'll be able to just live naked in the sunshine together. There will be no hassles with the police, because there won't be any police. The kids won't bother us, because there won't be any kids. We can set a studio up and just make our albums, swim about in the Aegean, and get stoned."

He still believed in the Beatles' dream.

The fact that Greece had just been taken control of by a band of fascist colonels didn't worry the four of them at all. In their wonderful cocooned anarchy, they could see little difference between the London drug squad and a military dictatorship. What did eventually stop them buying the island was an inept attempt by the Greek government's public relations board to cash in on the group's popularity.

While the Beatles were in Greece visiting their island, they were politely asked by a friendly tourist board man to take a look around a picturesque village on the mainland. As they walked onto the only street in the place, they were suddenly ambushed by hordes of waiting reporters, TV crews, and cameramen. The Beatles, in their attempt to seek refuge from the publicity hounds, had been bitterly disappointed.

"We might as well stay at home," said John.

Reality, as it had a way of doing, had caught up with them.

9

WHEN SHE WAS THERE, with her ready laugh and her quick, light step, there was joy; and when she was away, there was a lonely, raging emptiness which nothing could assuage. Eric Clapton was deeply, desperately, all-consumingly in love. Instead of playing guitar, he just dreamed about her all day and read gentle, romantic poems and novels. One book, in particular—Nizami's thousand-year-old Persian love story, *Layla and Majnun*—so moved him that he read it twice. The book told of a deep and tragic love between a young man and a young woman, a love which continued despite her marriage to another man. He liked that.

Although Eric's beautiful young girlfriend often stayed with him at Hurtwood Edge, his baronial hall near the village of Ewhurst, their relationship seemed to be based largely on a shared fondness for miscellaneous intoxicants.

Often he must have wished they were bonded more closely together because he would have been spared the heartache and soul-searching he felt now: Eric was in love with the wife of his best friend . . . Patti Harrison.

George had married Patti in 1966, when she was an actress and model best known for her appearance in a television advertisement for Smith's Crisps. Patti was the kind of girl

who causes car crashes every time she walked down the
street. With her silky blonde hair, dancing cat's eyes, and
long skirts, she had always been the center of attraction. But
her stunning appearance had more than once led to awkward
situations with George's friends.

The most embarrassing incident had been at a fancy-dress
party thrown by the Beatles for the launch of the *Magical
Mystery Tour* film. Patti, dressed as a belly dancer, giggled
with delight as almost every man in the room gazed longingly
at her ample charms. John Lennon—dressed as a Liverpool
greaser in a leather jacket and stovepipe pants—had steamed
up to her, ignoring George, and had turned on every iota of
his personality to the end of persuading her to join him
between the sheets. John's wife, Cynthia—dressed as a fairy-
tale princess—had fumed furiously until her friend, Lulu—
dressed as Shirley Temple, complete with lollypop—had
stormed indignantly up to John to ask him just what the hell
he thought he was doing. The scene set all the guests roaring
with laughter. After that, John had sheepishly returned to his
wife.

Eric knew his love was not returned and tried to come to
terms with it. But Patti led him on and encouraged his
adoration in order to reassure herself of her own attractive-
ness and to force George to pay more attention to her.

"She used me, you see," said Eric, "and I fell madly in love
with her."

Since the Beatles' break-up, George's interest in Hinduism
had begun to border on obsession. During George's first trip
to India in the Sixties, Ravi Shankar had introduced George
and Patti to his guru, Tat Buba, and they had spent two
months playing sitar and talking long into the night until all
the madness of the previous years could be seen in clear
perspective. The two of them stopped eating meat and eggs,
ceased drinking alcohol, and saw clearly the shallow far-
cicality of attempting to use drugs as a shortcut to spiritual
enlightenment.

George Harrison studying the sitar with Ravi Shankar

George's first desperate passion for India and her myriad philosophies had later matured into a quieter love, and he had begun to live his life loosely according to Hindu principles, with an unshakable belief in the law of *karma*— the doctrine of the inevitable consequences of every act we commit—which made his greatest pleasure giving his money away to anyone who came to him with a plausible request. He donated £5,000 a year to Release, the London charity which helps people who are in trouble because of drugs. He gave aid to a multitude of friends and other deserving causes. Later, he began to develop a deep interest in the Radha Krishna Temple. The Radha Krishna monks were disciples of a strict sect which forbade alcohol, vanity, and sex without the aim of producing children. During the last days of the Beatles, George had begun to meditate with them, often for an hour or more each day. He also helped them to produce a couple of records of their *mantras,* which he released through Apple.

He had even persuaded John for awhile to allow a few of the monks to live with him at Tittenhurst Park. ("I couldn't get any peace with all their bloody chanting," John said later.)

"Through Hinduism, I feel a better person," George explained. "I just get happier and happier. I now feel for a fact that I am unlimited, and I am more in control of my own physical body. The thing is, you go to an ordinary church and it's a nice feeling. They tell you about God, but they don't show you the way. They don't show you how to become Christ-conscious yourself. Hinduism is different."

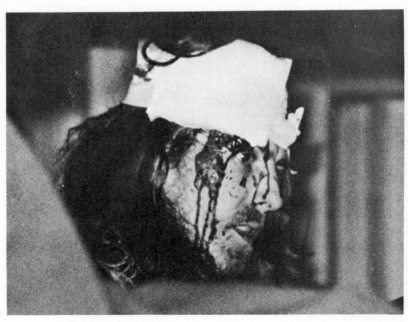

George being driven to the hospital following a car crash on February 29, 1972. Despite heavy bleeding, George was not seriously hurt

George had become a vegetarian, had given up drinking, smoking dope, and even, for the most part, cigarettes. Lately, he would sometimes meditate, cross-legged and insanely chanting his mantra, for fourteen hours or more at a stretch.

Patti was devoted to George, and was initially as fascinated by and dedicated to Hinduism as he was. But lately, she had felt hurt, as though the meditation was cutting her out of his life. She was twenty-six now and she wanted children, even if, as seemed increasingly likely, they would have to adopt. She still loved George very much.

The idea that Patti might leave him didn't even cross George's mind. With his album and single at the top of the hit parade in almost every country on earth, he had been hailed as the most important rock star of the Seventies and every day of his life now seemed crammed with excitement.

Aside from music and his quest for spiritual enlightenment, George's principle passion at this time was Friar Park, his palatial and astonishing new home. After the drug raids in 1969, he and Patti had been eager to move away. They no longer felt secure in their psychedelic bungalow. So they had searched for two years and finally, in the picturesque riverside town of Henley-on-Thames, they had stumbled upon Friar Park. The thirty-three acres of parkland were chest-high with weeds, the lakes were silted, and the house itself was a damp, decaying mess, but within minutes of their arrival, they looked at one another and knew they had to have it. Considering the estate's condition, it was terribly overpriced at $300,000, but the agent explained that this was because permission had been granted to demolish the old house and build an estate of valuable new houses in the grounds.

"That would be terrible, criminal," said George. He signed the contracts a few weeks later and immediately hired a team of builders plus ten full-time gardeners to begin the massive work of restoration.

"I want the place to look just the way it did when Queen Victoria came here for tea," he told them.

Though the house appeared to be centuries old, it had in fact been rebuilt a mere eighty years previously by a Victorian eccentric named Sir Frank Crisp, a lawyer who had been an advisor to the Liberal Party and whose guidance is said to have saved the Asquith government at the turn of the century.

Sir Frank poured much of his fortune into creating one of the most bizarre palaces in England—Friar Park. The main house was a happy mixture of French Renaissance and Gothic architecture which gave it a passing resemblance to Versailles. Door handles to the seventy-odd rooms were made from brass in the shape of monk's heads. He had a statue outside the house of a friar holding a frying pan riddled with holes captioned: "TWO HOLY FRIARS."

Similar jests were carved all over the house, such as "YESTERDAY, TODAY WAS TOMORROW. TOMORROW, TODAY WILL BE YESTERDAY," and: "MAKE TIME, SAVE TIME, WHILE TIME LASTS, ANY TIME'S NO TIME WHEN TIME'S PAST."

But it was in the gardens that Sir Frank Crisp had really indulged himself. Three lakes were built on slightly different levels. On summer evenings, Sir Frank would delight in inviting his guests to look at the view, while one of his gardeners punted slowly across the lake. Sir Frank would secretly signal to the man, who would deftly slip his punt from one lake to the next, and by crouching down in the boat, he would appear, from the house, to have vanished. Secret stepping-stones a quarter of an inch below the surface of the lake nearest the house allowed Sir Frank's butler to appear with a tray of drinks, apparently walking on water.

A faithful reproduction of the Alps stood in one corner of the garden—including a perfect, one hundred-foot-high replica of the Matterhorn. In the summer, 40,000 different types of flowers, trees, and shrubs were said to bloom in this section of the garden alone. There were also a series of caves linked by a mysterious underground river. Each cave had its own extraordinary character: the skeleton cave contained countless skeletons and distorting mirrors, the vine cave huge bunches of illuminated glass "grapes," the gnome cave was filled with more gnomes than a row of Surbiton gardens. Sir Frank's favorite cave was the "big cave," where he had a wishing well installed. While one looked down, a servant swiveled a handle until four heads appeared in turn—two men and two women—from whom one could choose his or her future sweetheart.

As well as restoring the house, George also became obsessed with Sir Frank Crisp, avidly reading every word that had been written about him. He was particularly intrigued by the man's duality, the contrast between his outrageous sense of humor and his piety. George was well aware of similar contradictions in his own outlook on life.

Even his own brothers, Harry and Peter Harrison, who George had invited to live with him in order to superintend the renovation program, found him hard to understand now. Harry, particularly, was less than delighted when George asked him if he would mind living in the gatekeeper's lodge with his family instead of in the main house. "It might look great from the outside," he thought the first time he looked around the place. "But it's really cramped and strange inside. I'd rather live in a nice, modern little house."

Harry, who was older than George and who had been a fitter before his famous little brother plucked him away from Liverpool, was perplexed at George's habit of retiring to a picturesque summerhouse on the grounds to meditate each day and by the dozens of strange, painted-faced, saffron-robed monks who wandered around the grounds chanting "Hare Krishna" to themselves.

George's growing involvement with devotees of the Krishna movement had led him to a meeting with His Divine Grace Guru Bhaktivedanta Swami, leader and founder of the International Society for Krishna Consciousness. Bhaktivedanta was a charismatic, awe-inspiring figure with a great, domed shaven head, a huge, sensuous mouth, and eyes which seemed to peer straight into the souls of all who met him. He was seventy-seven then and had attained the rare state of *prabhupad*—"the master at whose feet all other masters sit." He encouraged George, whenever possible, to rise with the dawn, to bathe in cold water, to meditate, and then to go to bed with the sun. One of the things George talked about with his guru was the seeming contradiction between his wealth and his search for spiritual enlightenment. But Bhaktivedanta had told him that it was right that he should earn money for the work he did and that only greed or selfishness was destructive.

At that time the movement's London headquarters was in a small house on Bury Place, off Oxford Street, but it was becoming increasingly apparent to George that they desperately needed a larger home for the thousands of devotees who were pouring into London from all over the world.

Bhaktivedanta had suggested the idea of purchasing a vast, fifty-five-room Elizabethan manor at Letchmore Heath, ten miles north of London, as a permanent headquarters for the movement. It would be possible, he thought, to raise the £250,000 needed if every devotee applied himself. In a typical gesture of impulsive generosity, George had insisted on paying for the house and its seventeen acres of land. It was, he felt, a paltry sum compared with the millions of dollars that *All Things Must Pass* and "My Sweet Lord" were grossing around the world.

More than one hundred devotees immediately moved into the new temple to settle into a regimen which consisted of rising at about three in the morning, taking a cold shower, then meditating or studying their holy book, the *Bhagavad-Gita,* until 8:15 when they ate a vegetarian breakfast. After that, they looked after the manor's herd of dairy cows, grew vegetables, made incense, or cooked and sewed.

George visited the house frequently on Sunday, which was a kind of open day when a huge vegetarian feast would be served to visitors and there would be music, dancing, acting, and films.

In the midst of all this, George still found time to work with people he admired—musicians like Jack Bruce, Billy Preston, Jackie Lomax and Doris Troy.

Nevertheless, George was still flattered when Eric Clapton asked him if he would help out on a song he was recording for his new album. What George didn't realize at the time was that Eric's new album was to be a hymn of love to Patti, a hymn that would profoundly affect her and which would strike at the very roots of her marriage to George.

Eric's desperate love was to produce, on this album, one of the most exquisite love songs ever recorded—"Layla." The lyrics were based on the story of *Layla and Majnun,* but everyone who knew the guitarist knew exactly who he was singing about.

By the time he flew to Miami to record the record, Eric was so wretched that he was blotting out reality with hash, wine, barbs, speed, even heroin—anything that would stroke or tear his mind away from his gloomy obsession with the wife of his best friend.

Despite his melancholia, Eric was enthusiastic when George told him of a concert he was planning to play on August 1, 1971, at Madison Square Garden in New York. The purpose of the concert, George explained, was to raise money for the starving people of Bangladesh. Bob Dylan had agreed to sing. And George had invited John, Paul, and Ringo to come along as well, together with a host of other brilliant musicians. The performance would also be recorded and filmed. It would be the concert of the decade. An excited Eric readily agreed to come—even if he had to crawl to Madison Square Garden on his hands and knees.

As it turned out, Eric very nearly had to—by the week of the concert, he had become heavily addicted to heroin. Before he flew out to New York for rehearsals, Eric arranged for supplies of the drug to be sent to him—only to discover on arrival that the stuff he was being supplied with was so heavily cut with talcum powder that he began to suffer chronic withdrawal symptoms. Only the offer of a friend's

Eric Clapton at Madison Square Garden

ulcer medicine—which just happened to be a heroin sub-
stitute called Methadone—made it possible for him to cease
shivering and perspiring so he could leave his hotel bed.

George had telephoned the other three Beatles to ask them
to join him on stage and they had all agreed. "Except,"
smiled Paul, "if I come, I want you to agree to let me out of
the partnership."

"I can't do that," said George. "That would be crazy. Forget
it."

John flew out to New York a few days before the concert.
He was very up, excited at the thought of appearing onstage
with the cream of the world's musicians. He would have the
joy of performing this time without the gut-wrenching terror
of having to hold the whole show together.

"Is there anything special you want Yoko to do?" he asked
George.

"Yes—I'd like her to enjoy watching the show."

Yoko was furious: how dare George tell John that he didn't
want her onstage. She began a near-hysterical argument
with George and John. After nearly an hour, John simply
turned his back and told his chauffeur to drive him to the
airport—he was returning to London. It just wasn't worth all
the hassle. Yoko followed, still reproaching him, the following day.

Ringo had agreed to play and so had several friends from
the old Apple band, Badfinger. The show represented a dash
of fire in the increasingly woeful life of Pete Ham, the group's
fair-haired leader. Pete was the member of the band who
really counted: the most talented songwriter, the most stylish
singer, and a musician who could switch effortlessly from
guitar to piano. With his cascade of fair hair, he was also the
one who seemed to attract girls to the band. Yet Pete had
always had reservations about what the Beatles had done to
Badfinger musically. "We're just going to sound like an
inferior Beatles," he protested as a frown clouded his sensitive features. He wanted to work harder at developing
Badfinger's own style of music. "The trouble is," he said soon

afterward, "that we have this image of being the new Beatles because of our records, our link with Apple, and the type of publicity we have been given. There will only be one Beatles. We're finding now that in Britain a lot of people won't come to see us because of this 'second-class Beatles' thing. It's all a drag." Sometimes Pete was thrown into a deep, all-obliterating depression by the situation in which he found himself.

But on August 1, as 20,000 people filed from a steamy New York night to sit excitedly before the seventy-foot-long stage, all problems were forgotten.

Ravi Shankar, who came from Bangladesh and who had asked George to arrange the concert, came on first. There was a brief interval and then George and Ringo were onstage together for the first time since the Beatles' last tour in 1966, five years before. With them were a vast array of musicians, among whom the crowd rapidly identified an emaciated and ill-looking Eric Clapton on guitar, plus Leon Russell and Billy Preston on keyboards.

Altogether, more than twenty musicians performed, but it was George in his white suit and tangerine shirt who dominated the show as he and the others thundered into "Wah-Wah," a track from his *All Things Must Pass* album, "My Sweet Lord," Billy Preston's "That's the Way God Planned it," Ringo's "It Don't Come Easy," Leon Russell leading "Jumpin' Jack Flash," and then George again with his classic Beatle hits "While My Guitar Gently Weeps," "Something," and "Here Comes the Sun."

"Here's another of our friends who you all know well," he told the audience, and then Bob Dylan slipped onto the stage, dazzling the cheering crowd with everything from "A Hard Rain's Gonna Fall" to "Blowin' in the Wind."

That night, at the after-the-show party in Jimmy Weston's Tavern, Phil Spector sang and played piano until dawn and even Dylan became tipsy.

Sadly, the euphoria of the night failed to survive the cold financial realities of the following days. Record companies jealously tried to delay release of the resultant triple album when they feared it would hurt sales of individual records by artists who had appeared at Madison Square Garden. Then both British and American tax agencies decided they had a stronger claim to the money than little children with swollen bellies and empty rice bowls.

George, desperate to resolve the situation, arranged a secret meeting with Patric Jenkin, Britain's chief financial undersecretary to the chancellor of the exchequer. Jenkin was implacable: the government was entitled to its cut and it was going to make quite certain it received it. George was hurt and angry—all his months of day-and-night labor were being exploited to help the grasping tax bureaus. He threatened Jenkin with leaving the country, taking his money elsewhere.

"That is your decision, Mr. Harrison," he was told.

Finally, on July 25, 1973, George pulled out his National Westminster Bank checkbook and calmly wrote a fresh, pink check for the sum of £1 million, payable to the Inland Revenue.

"And that," he said, "is the last time I get involved in anything like that."

10

JOHN'S BITTERNESS AT the snatching, mean-mouthed businessmen who had helped to destroy the Beatles, and the politicians and priests who had sneered at his campaign for peace, had bubbled over into an open hatred of the Establishment. Of course, his dislike and resentment had always been there—his anger against the Establishment was what had brought John and Yoko together in the first place. The first thing of Yoko's at an exhibition at John Duncan's Indica Gallery that had caught John's eye was an ordinary green apple—this was before he had even dreamed of Apple Corps. Ltd.—and beside it was a price tag for nearly $500. The wit, the simple satire against those who made fortunes from the wondrous creations of others appealed to him so much that he actually laughed aloud. There was also a high stepladder with apparently blank canvas affixed to the ceiling above it. Dangling from the edge of the canvas was a small magnifying glass on a chain. John climbed the ladder, picked up the glass, and peered myopically through it at a tiny word printed on the canvas. "YES," it said.

"So it was positive," said John later. "I felt relieved. It's a great relief when you get up the ladder and you look through the spyglass and it doesn't say: 'NO' or 'FUCK YOU' or something. It says 'YES.'"

He was excited then; although he hadn't met Yoko Ono in

person, he felt an empathy for her. The next exhibit of Yoko's John had gone to consisted of a board with the command: "HAMMER A NAIL IN." Beside the board lay a hammer and a box of nails. John, who had just been introduced to Yoko, asked out of courtesy of she would mind him bashing a nail in.

"I'd rather you didn't," she said. "The show doesn't start properly until tomorrow."

"He's a millionaire, you know," John Dunbar whispered in her ear. "One of the Beatles."

"OK, then," she told John. "If you are so rich, you can hammer a nail in if you pay me five shillings."

"I've got a better idea," John leered, putting on his broadest Scouse accent. "I'll give you an imaginary five shillings and hammer an imaginary nail in."

"And that's when we really met," he said later. "That's when we locked eyes and she got it and I got it. . . ."

For their peace campaigns John and Yoko now began to dress in fatigues, pose for photographs in sinister, military-style helmets, and began to preach revolution. As always, his state of mind was immediately transmuted into his music, and he produced a marching song for the revolution he so longed for. The anthem was called "Power to the People," and it was seized upon around the world as a rallying call by young people sick of President Nixon's evil escalation of the Vietnam war and of Britain's unseemly repression of the working people of Northern Ireland.

John was at once feted as the powerful new figurehead he was by Britain's left-wing would-be revolutionaries.

"The acid dream is over. That is what I am trying to tell them," he preached to Tariq Ali and Robin Blackburn in the extreme left-wing magazine, Red Mole .

"It seems to me that the students are now half-awake enough to try and wake up their brother workers. If you don't pass on your own awareness, then it closes down again. That is why the basic need is for the students to get in with the workers and convince them they are not talking gobbledygook. And of course it's difficult to know what the workers are really thinking because the capitalist press only quotes mouthpieces like Vic Feather anyway. . . ."

Squeezing Yoko's hand a little tighter, he went on: "Women are very important, too. We can't have a revolution that doesn't involve and liberate women. It's so subtle the way you're taught male superiority. It took me quite a long time to realize that my maleness was cutting off certain areas for Yoko. She's a red-hot liberationist and was quick to show me where I was going wrong, even though it seemed to me that I was just acting naturally. That's why I'm always interested to know how people who claim to be radical treat women. . . ."

John himself had taken a long time to reach this statement of sexual enlightenment. John had once sat spellbound as Yoko spilled out to him in shimmering sentences the reasons why women were biologically superior to men. Women, she said, had developed to a higher state than men so that, in general, they were more likely to have qualities of telepathy, sensitivity, caring, and gentleness than men; qualities which were far more relevant to the world in the twentieth century than the masculine qualities of aggression, ambition, and curiosity. Women, on the average, live longer than men; they need less food and are more able to bear pain.

He himself had long been confused by his attitude to women: he had loved his mother, Julia, with a desperate, reverential passion; Mimi had left him bewildered but he felt indebted to her; Cynthia had been so remote. In his teens, in Liverpool, he had frequently kicked and insulted his girl-friends so that more than one of them had been stung to screech at him: "Don't take it out on me, Lennon—just because your mother is dead!"

Then Yoko had clarified his thoughts, had ordered his chaotic attitude toward women. Everything she said made such perfect sense to him, swept away so much psychological clutter.

"I think we must make the workers aware of the really

unhappy position they are in, break the dream they are surrounded by. They think they are in a wonderful, free-speaking country, they've all got cars and tellies and they don't want to think there's anything more to life: they are prepared to let the bosses run them, to see their children fucked-up in school. They're dreaming someone else's dream, it's not even their own.

"They should realize that the blacks and the Irish are being harassed and repressed and that they will be next. As soon as they start being aware of all that, we can really begin to do something. The workers can start to take over.

"But we'd also have to infiltrate the army, too, because they are well trained to kill us all. We've got to start all this from where we, ourselves, are oppressed. I think it's false, shallow, to be giving to others when your own need is great. The idea is not to comfort people, not to make them feel better, but to make them feel worse, to put before them constantly the degradations and humiliations they go through to get what they call a living wage. . . ."

Inevitably, his opponents were not slow to point laughingly to the obvious contradiction between his words and his enjoyment of his Rolls-Royce and Tittenhurst Park.

"Look," he said later, "they knock me for saying 'Power to the People' and say that no one section should have power. Crap. The people aren't a section. The people means everyone. I think that everyone should own everything equally and that the people should own part of the factories and they should have some say in who is the boss and who does what. It's the same as students should be able to select teachers.

"It might be like communism, but I don't really know what real communism is. There is no real communist state in the world, you must realize that Russia isn't. It's a fascist state. The socialism I talk about is a British socialism, not where some daft Russian might do it, or the Chinese might do it. That might suit them. Us, we'd have a nice socialism here. A British socialism."

John's friends, the people he had known since the days at

art school in Liverpool, heard his words and smiled. Even in his teens, John had had a streak of nihilism in his nature so that he had often said he wished there would be a war or an earthquake so he could rape and pillage to his heart's content. It was this iconoclastic side to John's nature which had been an integral part of the Beatles' appeal to many people.

There was also an irreconcilable difference between John's brave words and his attitude towards the workers he himself had employed at Apple—which was, of course, a straightforward capitalist enterprise, whichever way one looked at it. As Paul's case for dissolution of the Beatles' partnership lumbered slowly through the courts, John became increasingly vehement in his attitude towards his former employees. They were, he said, hustlers and spongers.

He was less vociferous, though, when McCartney's lawyer revealed that Klein had been convicted of ten tax offenses in New York the previous year.

"Well, anyone whose record is as bad as that can't be all bad," was John's only comment.

However, Klein rapidly sprang to his own defense, pointing out that the Beatles had earned more than nine million pounds—exclusive of their songwriting royalties—in the year and a half for which he had managed them. This was more than they had managed to earn in the entire six years before he took over their affairs, he said.

Nevertheless, Mr. Justice Stamp, who was hearing the case, appeared suspicious of Klein. He referred to the "enormous" sums of money paid to Klein's company, ABKCO. He said he could see grounds for Paul's mistrust and on March 13 he placed Apple's affairs into the hands of the receiver.

The Beatles' fight, said the newspapers, was over. In fact, it was only just beginning.

When Paul recorded his first album, he was so unbalanced

that he had been unable to face working with anyone—but the hostile reception the record had received had decided him; next time, he would have a little more help.

John had attained bliss through working with Yoko, Paul seemed to decide. Very well—he would work with Linda. She had protested that she hadn't played a musical intrument since her school days, but he told her not to worry, he'd just teach her a few simple chords on the electric organ—things even a ten-year-old child would be able to cope with. It would be a relief, he felt, to be able to talk about music with Linda without her eyes glazing over.

There are still girls in New York, girls with weary shadows under their eyes and black roots to their blonde hair, who will tell you that Linda Eastman was the uncrowned empress of Sixties groupies. But their vitriolic acclaim is the acclaim of good-time girls for whom the good times are long over. Linda Eastman may have been pursued and feted by innumerable rock stars—but she never was a groupie.

Even at school, she was much adored by young men; though not a classical beauty, there is something about Linda's self-deprecating sense of humor, her original way of looking at things, and the self-assured, measured way in which she moves that make her sexy and desirable in a way in which many more photogenic girls are not.

She came from a wealthy middle-class family with three homes—including a lavish apartment on Park Avenue. Her father, Lee Eastman, was a successful show business lawyer with a widely coveted art collection and her mother, too, was independently wealthy.

Linda learned to ride, became an expert on contemporary art, and looked all set to join New York's thriving café society scene. Until, that was, her mother died in an airplane disaster shortly after Linda's eighteenth birthday. Linda was devastated: she had been close to her mother and had leaned on her heavily. For a few months, she had wandered around in a state of dazed shock, then, suddenly, she had told her father that she wanted to marry. Her husband-to-be was a geophysicist named John See and, shortly after the wedding, the pair of them moved to Colorado. They rapidly produced a beautiful daughter whom they named Heather. And then they discovered that they bored one another to distraction. When Linda could stand no more, she bundled her things into a couple of old suitcases, tucked Heather under her arm, and flew to think things over in Tucson, then home to New York.

A few phone calls to old friends rapidly produced a job as a receptionist with the tweedy *Town & Country* magazine, but Linda rapidly became restless once again. Her chance to break away from routine came when an invitation arrived at her office for a representative to meet the Rolling Stones onboard a motor yacht on the Hudson River.

Linda filched the invitation, then slipped her Pentax into her handbag and set off for the party. Mick Jagger was captivated by her. He had been under enormous pressure in England, had recently suffered a nervous breakdown, and he found Linda's wit and her fresh openness a delightful contrast to the cloying, grabbing women he had, until then, been involved with. Linda's pictures of the Stones were widely published and she became a close friend of Jagger's. Subsequently, she wrote an article for a New York girl's magazine about her "night with Mick." The two of them had whiled away the small hours phoning different radio stations to request records, she said. A place on Linda's bathroom wall was subsequently given to a blow-up of a photograph a press photographer had taken of her with the head Stone.

Then Eric Burden arrived in New York with the Animals, and she began going everywhere with him. The two of them were snapped at a nightclub in Harlem by a photographer from the black magazine *Ebony*; they went together to see Otis Redding in Central Park.

After that, the gossips were linking her with almost every celebrity who arrived in town. She went to the Delmonico

Hotel in New York to photograph Warren Beatty and immediately she was rumored to be enjoying a torrid love affair with him.

When a new rock theater called the Fillmore East opened in New York in 1968, she was invited to become the house photographer. Though she wasn't paid anything, the job gave her the chance to take some extraordinarily candid photographs of the rock stars she adored. Janis Joplin, Jim Morrison, Pete Townshend, Jackson Browne, and countless others came under her zoom lens. Certainly, one or two of them became special to her and she enjoyed close friendships with them.

Sometimes, too, her method of working gave rise to much spurious speculation: "I've always liked to spend a day with someone if I'm going to take their photograph," she said. "If you have a really nice day, having lunch together, going to the zoo maybe, the pictures can't fail to turn out well."

And then came Paul McCartney: "I was quite shameless, really," she giggles. "I was with somebody else at the Bag O'Nails Club in Soho to see Georgie Fame and the Blue Flames and I saw Paul at the other side of the room. He looked so beautiful that I made up my mind I would have to pick him up."

After an hour of winsome glances and coy smiles, Paul got the message and he spoke briefly with her. But it certainly wasn't love at first sight and, to Linda's disappointment, he didn't ask her to see him again. They met a few weeks later at a press luncheon to launch the *Sgt. Pepper* album, but still Paul didn't seem particularly interested.

When they met for the third time, Paul had come to New York with John in May 1968 to announce the formation of Apple. Linda could see him looking at her, but he was surrounded by so many people that she couldn't possibly talk quietly with him. At length, in desperation, she slipped a piece of paper with her phone number on it into his hand. He called her later that evening and she stayed the night at a friend's apartment, where John and Paul were living during their visit.

After that, he couldn't stop thinking about her and, a few weeks later, he asked her to come with him on a business trip he was making to Los Angeles. She adored him, made no secret of the fact that she was a fan, that his slightest whim was her command, and he reveled in the love and attention that this woman heaped upon him. But his memory of her began to fade when he returned to London—now that he had broken with Jane, he was enjoying the torrid love life of his bachelor days once again.

Linda fretted and talked endlessly to her friends about what she should do. "Go to London," one girlfriend told her. "Pretend you've got a photographic assignment and then just call him. At least you'll know one way or the other where you stand."

So Linda had gone to London and within days she was ensconsed in Paul's psychedelically painted house in St. John's Wood. The fans who had always been so devoted to Paul had made it apparent that they did not approve of Paul's new girlfriend and, later, wife. They, in effect, launched a vicious hate campaign against her. Once, shortly before their wedding, she received a letter which warned her that if she didn't leave Paul alone acid would be thrown into her face. And when she walked past the fans, they would taunt her with infantile insults like: "Hairy legs," or "Ugly face."

"I just wasn't ready for all of it," said Linda. "I married Paul because we loved one another and I didn't even think about the attacks that were going to be made on me. All I could do was just go on being myself and let people either take me or leave me."

Later, about the time of the Beatles break-up, the fans found a way of breaking into Paul's house—via a dog-door he had installed for Martha—when he and Linda went out. At first, they had simply looked around and taken photographs of one another, but lately they had taken to stealing Linda's clothes or ripping her irreplaceable pictures to shreds.

Linda was about to find that her new career as a musician was not going to be easy either. She and Paul flew to New York to find a drummer. Though Paul was good on the drums himself, he felt that it would be healthier to have the stimulus of someone with some fresh ideas. He held auditions in a dilapidated basement with appalling acoustics amid conditions of stringent secrecy.

"This is a bit weird," Denny Seiwell thought when he arrived. Seiwell had earned a good reputation as a session drummer and he wasn't used to having to prove himself any more. He was earning hundreds of dollars a week playing for countless bands in a dozen or more studios each month.

"OK," said Paul. "There's the drum-kit—now play it."

"This is stupid," Denny thought to himself as he settled into the seat. "These drums are rubbish and he's not even going to accompany me."

He'd played the best way he knew how, noticing the look of approbation in McCartney's eyes when he gave a hasty tom-tom solo. Next day, Paul told him he had got the gig. They recorded the album together at high speed, hampered only by Paul's painstaking efforts to persuade Linda to sing harmonies or play keyboards.

"What on earth is she doing singing with Paul McCartney?" thought Denny.

The resultant album was called *Ram* and the cover photograph showed Paul grasping a ram by the horns on his farm—he had bought four hundred or more acres now and he was beginning to take sheep breeding seriously.

The record contained some strong tracks, including "Uncle Albert," "Heart of the Country," "Monkberry Moon Delight," and "The Back Seat of My Car." Paul was optimistic that it would force the critics who had been so unpleasant about his first LP to eat humble pie. He always read reviews and articles about himself avidly. Even as a teen-ager, he had been desperately concerned about what people thought of him—quite unlike the other Beatles—so that if someone said, for example, that his trousers looked silly, he would feel miserable all day.

Paul pounced eagerly on the music papers as they plopped through the letter-box in the week after review copies of the record had been sent out.

Hastily, he thumbed his way through the first one to the record section. There it was: "*Ram*— PAUL MCCARTNEY."

"How do you tell an ex-Beatle," he read, "that he has made a lousy album?"

He hurled the paper to the floor in disgust. Later, he refused to read that particular publication for many weeks. Most of the reviews were similar—and several turned into personal attacks on Paul and Linda. The record wasn't really *that* bad. It was simply the first chance most writers had had to get their own backs on Paul for—as they saw it—breaking up the Beatles.

John had disliked the album, too. There was one song in particular, called "Too Many People," which flatly decried the great number of people preaching their beliefs. John knew exactly where that particular dart had been aimed.

Five months later with the release of *Imagine*—far and away the most brilliant album of John's post-Beatle career—Lennon gleefully retaliated, first by including a photograph of himself holding a pig by the ears—a direct and insulting parody of Paul's *Ram* album cover. He also included a bitter attack on Paul in his song "How Do You Sleep"—a song on which George Harrison had readily agreed to play guitar—with lyrics that said Paul had done nothing but "Yesterday," declaring Paul's work to be Muzak. Surely, John cynically taunted, Paul must have learned something in all those years they were together.

Paul was shaken by the attack on him by John and the critics. He had decided he would have to form a proper band. He desperately needed musicians he could bounce ideas off.

He phoned Denny Seiwell to see if Denny would consider teaming up with him permanently.

"Would I what?" asked Seiwell excitedly. He and his wife, Monique, were on a plane the same day, and they soon moved in to a small crofter's cottage a few miles down the lane from Paul's farm.

Next Paul decided to recruit Denny Laine, who had once been the leader of the Moody Blues. Paul and Denny had been close friends in the faroff days when the Beatles and the Moodies were rivals, and Paul had said in more than one interview that he thought Denny was one of the best rock singers and guitarists in Great Britain. Laine had sung with chilling intensity on "Go Now!", the Moodies' first big hit, and he had also been successful with a solo single called "Say You Don't Mind." Denny had little sense of ambition, however, and he was far happier laughing with friends than striving to make a fortune. After leaving the Moody Blues, he spent a year living in a shack in Andalusia, Spain, learning to play flamenco guitar.

When Paul phoned, he was so broke that he was sleeping on a mattress on the floor in his manager's office in Mayfair. But he was putting together songs for a solo album and he was completely unperturbed by his lack of cash.

"Yeah," he agreed. "Yeah, I'd like to play with you, Paul. It would be fun."

When Denny arrived at the farm, Paul rolled a few joints. They sat round with Linda and Denny Seiwell, growing quietly stoned and laughing about their crazy old days until Denny had passed out from sheer travel exhaustion.

The following day, Paul had shown Denny around the farm—the part that most impressed him was the greenhouse full of tomato and marijuana plants. They had then gone into a barn next to the farmhouse to jam together. The result, they all agreed, was magic.

Paul was so desperate to make up for the disastrous *Ram* album that he booked the band straight into a recording studio. He wanted to capture their freshness and fire before all the energy was rehearsed out of them.

"Bob Dylan has been talking about getting away from overdubbing and back to simplicity," he thought. So they experimented with just rushing through their songs, often without even giving the engineer time to correctly set up his equipment, and the whole project was finished in less than two weeks. The resulting record was rush-released to reviews even more vitriolic than those for *Ram*.

"McCartney is a spent force," the critics said. "Third-rate suburban pop." Even the fans were unimpressed and the record sold less copies than his first two. It was the nadir of Paul's career.

Paul realized he was losing touch with his audience, with the fans; he was no longer certain what they wanted to hear. For the first time since the Beatles' farewell tour of 1966, he determined to go out on the road. Denny had advised an extra guitarist to beef up their sound, and Henry Mc-Cullough, a taciturn Irishman who had played with Joe Cocker's barnstorming Grease Band, was recruited.

In September 1971, after Linda had been rushed into the hospital to give birth to her third child, Paul and Linda argued back and forth about names for the baby. At the same time, Paul began to toss around names for the band as well.

"How about Wings of Angels?" he said. "Or Wings of Eagles?"

"How about just Wings?" asked Linda. "It's got a nice sound to it. Like Beatles."

Paul agreed. All Paul had to do now was to learn how to use his Wings to fly again.

Ringo was becoming bored, much to his surprise. He had always thought he would be happy when the Beatles ended, but it hadn't felt quite the way he hoped it would. He loved playing with the three children and he had enjoyed drumming with George and John on their solo projects, but he rather hoped that a worthwhile film part would come along.

Maureen was still devoted to him: when he said jokingly that he rather fancied having a blonde for a change, she had asked the hairdresser to bleach her beautiful, long, dark, shiny hair. When he said he was tired of living out at Esher, they had moved to a new £75,000 mansion just down the road from Lulu and her husband, Maurice Gibb of the Bee Gees, beside Hampstead Golf Course.

But still something seemed to missing from his life. He began to drink a little more than he had in the past.

11

"I WANT TO SEE MY BABY!" Yoko had screamed at John. "Kyoko is mine. She should be living with us. Why hasn't anybody done anything to help us find her?"

Tony Cox, Yoko's ex-husband, had been wonderful at first: "He's the best babysitter we could wish for," Yoko had joked. Tony had been so enamored of John that he had even made a film of John and Yoko at home in Tittenhurst Park. Although Kyoko lived with Tony, she sometimes would stay with John and Yoko for a day or two.

Things had changed radically on the day of Kyoko's seventh birthday, however, when she asked her father to watch the film John had given to her as a birthday present: the film showed Kyoko and John splashing naked in a bath together.

Though the film was obviously innocent, it seemed to disturb Tony so much that he decided to remove Kyoko from John and Yoko's influence. Quietly, he packed his and her things into a few suitcases and flew with her to the sunny Mediterranean holiday island of Majorca, where he rented a small villa.

"OK," said John. "We'll go after her and bring her back."

Grimly, they checked into their hotel on Majorca, ignoring the curious stares of the thronging tourists. Then they took a car to Tony's villa. They waited outside until they saw Kyoko

145

playing by herself in the sunshine. She was pleased to see them at first, though confused when they told her that they didn't want to see her father and that she was to come in the car with them to their hotel.

John and Yoko's lawyer had advised them that if they were to "kidnap" Kyoko, then the courts would allow Yoko to keep the child. Tony was distraught when he discovered his daughter missing and immediately called in the police. Within hours, John, Yoko, Tony, and Kyoko were hauled before a judge in a dusty old courtroom close to the yacht harbor in the island's capital of Palma. The judge, a kindly man who spoke fluent English, listened patiently to what each of the three adults wished to say. When they had finished, the judge, smiling at Kyoko, took her by the hand and led her into a small anteroom at the back of the court. When the two were out of earshot of the rest, the judge asked Kyoko: "And who would you like to live with—do you want to go with your mummy or your daddy?"

"My daddy," said Kyoko.

"Then so you shall."

Tony and Kyoko had promptly flown on to the States while John and Yoko had returned to London, wretched with anger and frustration, to again consult with their lawyers. This time, they were advised that they would have to travel to the Virgin Islands, to the same court where Yoko and Tony had been divorced, if they were to obtain a custody order. If that was granted, all they would have to do would be to fly on to New York, present Tony with the order; then—if he refused to comply with the order—he would be jailed.

There was barely a query in the Virgin Islands as the court happily awarded Yoko custody of Kyoko. Bubbling over with the thrill of victory, the two of them boarded a jet to New York.

It was September, 1971, and neither John nor Yoko could have had the slightest inkling that he was destined never again to see the lush, green England he so loved.

During Christmas of 1971, it was virtually impossible to turn on a radio in the United States without hearing John and Yoko's gentle and idealistic Christmas carol, "Happy Xmas (War Is Over)." But for one man, the song provoked only a bitterly ironic smile. While John and Yoko had been singing to the world of a new era of peace and understanding, they had also been secretly arranging legal plans which would land Tony Cox in a prison cell.

While John and Yoko were in the Virgin Islands obtaining their custody order, Tony had flown to Houston, Texas, where his beautiful new wife, Melinda, had been brought up. They set up home together, changed Kyoko's name to Rosemary, and applied to Houston Domestic Relations Court for legal custody. Tony had become a born-again Christian in his travels and his appeal to Judge Peter Solito was heavily reinforced by quotations from the Bible and references to Christ.

The good judge gave Mr. and Mrs. Cox temporary custody, adding that his decision would overrule any order made by the Virgin Islands courts.

Not surprisingly, Tony was worried that there would be a second kidnap attempt. So Judge Solito ordered that, although Yoko could have extensive access to Kyoko, she would have to pay a $20,000 surety into the court to ensure Kyoko's return.

It was later agreed that John and Yoko could take Kyoko away with them for ten days at Christmas, but that they should first spend a weekend with her in Houston to give her a chance to get to know them again.

John and Yoko were living now in a small basement flat in New York's Greenwich Village. On December 18—exactly as instructed by the judge—they flew to Houston to spend their first weekend with Kyoko.

"I'm sorry," Tony told them when they arrived, "but I'm not going to leave her alone with you."

John and Yoko were furious. They immediately called in

their powerful team of lawyers. "It's a clear-cut case of contempt of court," they were advised. "You can have him sent to jail."

On December 22, just as "Happy Xmas (War Is Over)" settled at the top of the charts, Tony was led, kicking and screaming, to a jail cell. "If any Christians are hearing my voice," he yelled, "I hope you will all pray for me."

The story was not over yet, however. Tony was released on a $5,000 bond the following day, and on Christmas Eve, he fled with Melinda and Kyoko.

Though John and Yoko hired a team of private detectives, they were unable to find any trace of them. Eventually, the Houston court reversed its earlier decision and awarded custody to Yoko. But it was too late: John and Yoko both realized at last that Kyoko was happy living with her father. She would never live with them again unless they really did kidnap her. Kyoko simply disappeared from their lives— never to be seen again.

Oddly enough, John showed little such interest in the welfare of his own son, Julian, who was left to live in Wales with Cynthia.

"I'm just sort of a figure in the sky," he was to confess years later. "But he's obliged to communicate with me, even when he probably doesn't want to."

"I'm not going to lie to Julian. Ninety percent of the people on this planet, especially in the West, were born out of a bottle of whiskey on a Saturday night, and there was no intent to have children. So ninety percent of us—that includes everybody—were accidents. I don't know anybody else who was a planned child. All of us were 'Saturday night specials.' Julian is in the majority, along with me and everybody else."

One of the loves of John's life at this time did not require a court order to pursue—New York City. John had been through New York several times with the Beatles, though then he had seen little but hotel rooms and concert halls. Yoko opened his eyes to the steamy delights of the most potent city on earth.

"I should have been born in Greenwich Village," he bubbled. "Paris was the center of the artistic world in the eighteenth century, then it was London, and now it is New York. New York is the center of the artistic and creative world.

"If I'd been living in the days of the Roman Empire, I'd have been living in Rome. Now New York is what Rome was then. I'd love it, for all its dirt and all its decay."

A few days after John and Yoko arrived, they had been telephoned by Jerry Rubin, a bright young radical politician who had been one of the defendants in the "Chicago Seven" political trial. He introduced them to his left-wing friend, Abbie Hoffman, and suddenly John and Yoko were plunged into the maelstrom of American political extremism. John was overjoyed: more than anything he wanted to feel involved, at the center of life in New York. After the years of isolation in Tittenhurst Park, it was like throwing himself back into the madness of his Liverpool adolescence. Better still, people here left him alone, he could actually walk into a shop or a restaurant without starting a near-riot.

When Jerry Rubin asked John to appear at a demonstration at the University of Michigan calling for the release from jail of the radical poet John Sinclair, he had been happy to oblige.

Sinclair had already served two years of a ten-year prison sentence for giving two joints to an undercover policewoman. Of course, his real crime was not possessing drugs but posing an illusory threat to the paranoid Nixon administration. Sinclair had founded the White Panthers and he had been a little too strident in his condemnation of America's corrupt role in Vietnam. Shortly after John's appearance at the demonstration, massive publicity and a nationwide outcry persuaded the government to free Sinclair on a legal technicality.

John and Yoko also became embroiled in the aftermath of a

riot at New York's Attica State Prison, a riot which left forty-three people—many of them guards—dead. John castigated the authorities for the way in which the situation had been handled—on nationwide television shows, on recordings, and at a benefit rally. In the midst of all this, John and Yoko even managed to find some time to campaign on behalf of downtrodden American Indians.

In a nation which was becoming increasingly polarized, many people, not surprisingly, became irritated by John and Yoko's meddling in the political affairs of a country where they were, after all, merely guests. Several newspapers carried articles asking them exactly what they thought they were up to, and there was aggressive heckling when John and Yoko were interviewed on the nationwide "David Frost Show."

John seemed unperturbed. He and Yoko bought a small loft building near their old Greenwich Village apartment and Yoko staged one of her bizarre exhibitions under the logo, "THIS IS NOT HERE." "PRIDE OF PLACE" was signified by a rusty old Volkswagen car which Andy Warhol had given them; another exhibit included an empty flowerpot with the caption: "IMAGINE THE FLOWERS."

They also began to write a monthly column for an underground magazine called *Sundance*.

"To the hardhats who think they don't have the power to free themselves from the tyranny and suppression of the capitalists," John wrote in one column, "it's not their power or money that is controlling you, as is generally believed. Their power depends on your fear and apathy."

John poured his sincere but naïve political anger into an album of songs about Angela Davis, John Sinclair, the IRA, prisons, and the Feminist movement. It was called *Sometimes in New York City* and it was, without doubt, the worst musical and lyrical disaster of his career. Just as Paul's songs had often sounded coy and slushy without John, so John now in his overindulgence became mawkish, tuneless, and charmless. Critics tore the record to shreds, and it sold

John and Yoko in New York in 1973

only a fraction as many copies as John's previous LP, *Imagine*.

The nearly seven hundred students in the hall had on their faces but one visage: stunned astonishment. They had come to their ordinary evening dance at Leeds University expecting to see one of the multitude of local groups playing the usual rhythm and blues and Beatles' hits. But here, instead, stepping out on the rickety wooden stage, looking even taller and more glorious than he had in all those films and photographs which had provided the focal point of their adolescence, was Paul McCartney.

"Evening," said Paul when his band had settled into the cramped space behind him. "We're going to kick off with a little song called 'Wildlife.' One, two, three. . . ."

Nothing happened. Paul, with a slight hesitation, began again.

"One, two three. . . ."

Still there was nothing. Paul turned around to glower at Linda, who was supposed to be kicking the song off with a few simple chords on her electric piano.

"I've forgotten the chords," she mouthed at him, glassy-eyed with fear.

The audience began to giggle in a slightly embarrassed, not unsympathetic way.

"OK, Linda," said Paul with remarkable restraint, as he turned around to help her. "Just put this finger on C, that one on F-sharp, like this, that's right, and then you'll remember the rest. . . ."

The audience relaxed and began to laugh out loud. This was clearly a new version of that zany Beatle humor they had all read about.

"OK, this time we're really going to do it. One, two, three. . . ."

And the concert began.

That night, as they smoked a joint together in their caravan, Linda broke down and wept.

"I feel totally out of place," she sobbed. "Everyone is so down on me."

Henry McCullough and Denny Seiwell had tried hard to disguise their fury but—after years of slogging their way through the music business jungle—it was clear that they found it galling to have to work together with an untrained girl on keyboards, just because she happened to be the boss's wife.

"Look," Paul told her. "If you look at any group or musician, there has to be a time when they were learning. George Martin didn't want Ringo to play on our first Beatles' record because he thought he wasn't good enough, and Ringo must have felt like giving up then.

"But he stuck it out and pretty soon he became a great drummer. Everyone has got to start somewhere. Anyway, I like the innocence that your playing brings to the band. It stops us becoming like the Beatles—too slick and clever."

Wings began their clandestine tour of British universities in February of 1972. They packed dogs, children, roadies, wives, and girlfriends into a rented Avis truck and a caravan and simply set off toward Nottingham University. After all, it seemed as good a place as any to begin a tour. They would park outside and send their roadie, Trevor Jones, in to see if he could fix a gig up for them.

The following lunchtime, eight hundred curious students paid fifty pence each to file into their hall to see Paul McCartney's new band. The show was a complete triumph and afterwards, in the caravan, Paul doled out the profits among the musicians.

This, he thought, was one of the best bits of all—actually seeing $100 or $150 in their hands at the end of the show instead of all the huge checks stumbling their ever-decreasing way through the hands of avaricious lawyers and accountants. For the first time since the Beatles' break-up, he was beginning to feel happy. The tour of universities lasted two weeks. As far as Paul was concerned, it could have gone on for two months. He dashed around bright-eyed, losing weight, for all the world like the boy-Beatle he had been in Liverpool.

Better still, he had finally become friendly with John again. The two of them had met up secretly in New York. At first, after all the musical and newspaper insults, they had both been embarrassed.

"It was the first time we had seen each other for two years," Paul told a friend. "But we got talking and it was really good. The vibes were right. The odd thing was that John and Yoko were just like me and Linda. They felt the same about music and politics and we had the same thoughts about Ireland—like how wrong the British government is to go in and crush the people like they are doing."

Liverpool is a city with a huge Irish working-class population, and both John and Paul numbered Irishmen among their ancestors, so they had grown up steeped in the folk-law mystique and romance of the IRA. In that January of 1972, the fracas between the Republicans and the British Army had erupted into open warfare, culminating in the Bloody Sunday of January 30, where 13 civilians were massacred by paratroopers after a banned civil rights march in Londonderry's Bogside.

Two days after the incident, as commentators seethed and argued about what should and should not have been done, Paul poured his own bitterness into a song called "Give Ireland Back to the Irish." The record was on sale within a month and—despite being banned by the BBC—it reached number sixteen in the charts.

John pumped thousands of pounds into a protest film entitled *The Luck of the Irish,* which depicted the IRA as heroic freedom fighters.

Toward the end of Wings' university tour, Paul's zest proved so infectious that even Linda was beginning to enjoy herself: "We've only been playing together for five days," she

Paul, Linda and their friend Cilla Black (center)

told a reporter from *Melody Maker*. "And already I have confidence in the band. So far, audience response has been good. Surprisingly, perhaps, I am enjoying these one-night appearances—it's like a touring holiday. If we wake up one morning and decide that we don't want to go to, say, Hull, we don't have to! With an organized tour, your freedom is limited. This is the only way to do it. Eric Clapton once said that he would like to play from the back of a caravan, but he never got around to it. Well, we have. We've no managers or agents, just we five and the roadies. We're just a gang of musicians touring around."

The tour, coupled with the passion of "Give Ireland Back to the Irish," had done much to repolish Paul's tarnished image when in May he chose, inexplicably, to commit a sort of musical *hara-kiri* by setting the banal lyrics of the childrens' nursery rhyme "Mary Had a Little Lamb" to a lilting new melody. When the song aired on British radio stations, the critics went for the throat. "So the once-great Paul McCartney has fallen to tripe like this?" they scoffed.

"You see, I do things that aren't necessarily very carefully thought out," Paul explained to interviewers later. "Now, you know, I've just got three kids over the last few years, and, when I am sitting at home playing at the piano, my audience a lot of the time is the kids. I just wrote that one up, the words were already written, you know, I just found out what the words to the nursery rhyme were. I thought it was all very deep and all very nice. I see now, you know, that it wasn't much of a record. That's all. It just didn't really make it as a record, and that's what tells, the black plastic."

In any case, the earthiest rocker of them all, Pete Townshend, the leader of the Who, had told Paul his daughter loved the record. Paul at least had the appreciation of the children he had written the music for in the first place to console himself.

The song vividly reflected Paul's lifelong desire to make music for everyone who would listen. He had no time for the purist pomposity of bands like the Rolling Stones and Led Zeppelin who seemed to insist on making music exclusively for streetwise kids. Paul was always prepared to play what he thought the person he was singing to wanted to hear.

12

FOR ALL JOHN'S PROSELYTIZING and sloganeering, in many ways he appeared to have become a pawn in Jerry Rubin's game of radical politics. Rubin and his friends realized that John could be used to attract thousands of new supporters. His ex-Beatle status made him one of the few men in the country who had open access to any television show he wished to appear on.

The government's internal security officers prepared a long, confidential memo in January, 1971, in which they pointed out John's association with this band of political activists.

"These people had been strong advocates of the program to dump Nixon," they warned. The memo went on to report that the group had "devised a plan to hold rock concerts in various primary election states to stimulate eighteen-year-old registration, to press for legalization of marijuana, to finance radical activities, and to recruit persons to come to San Diego during the Republican National Convention in August, 1972. These individuals are the same persons who were instrumental in disrupting the Democratic National Convention in Chicago in 1968."

The goverment felt that these radicals intended to use John Lennon as a drawing card to promote the success of rock festivals and rallies, pouring tremendous amounts of money into the coffers of the New Left. As a result, the government decided to terminate the Lennons' visas.

John and Yoko, of course, knew nothing of the memo and so in January, 1972, they blithely asked their lawyer, Leon Wildes, if he could arrange for their visas—which expired on March 1—to be extended. Normally, extensions are a mere formality and they are granted to anyone who has sufficient funds to support himself. But this time, Mr. Wildes was told no extension would be possible—the Lennons would have to leave the country by March 15. The reason given for the refusal was John's British conviction for possession of cannabis.

Mr. Wildes immediately applied for a residential visa in an effort to stall things indefinitely, but to no avail. On April 18, deportation proceedings were begun against John and Yoko. They arrived at the Immigration Service building both dressed identically in conservative blue suits with neat matching ties. A furious legal argument ensued, during which Mr. Wildes drew skillful parallels between John Lennon and Yoko Ono's deportation, and the way in which America had driven an earlier British genius—Charlie Chaplin—from her shores. Though John and Yoko were not granted visas, Mr. Wildes's eloquent plea resulted in permission for John and Yoko to stay in America pending an appeal.

At once, the case became a *cause célèbre*. New York's mayor, John Lindsay, protested: "The only question which is raised against these people is that they speak out with strong and critical voices on major issues of the day. If this is the motive underlying the unusual and harsh action taken by the Immigration and Naturalization Service, then it is an attempt to silence Constitutionally protected 'First Amendment' rights. A grave injustice," he added, "is being perpetrated."

Lord Harlech, Britain's former ambassador to the United States, agreed: "As a lifelong friend of the United States of America, I reject the suggestion that the most powerful democratic country in the world, whose whole *Constitution* is based on individual freedom and human rights, could believe for one moment that it might be subverted by the presence of a single young artist."

Others who pleaded for John and Yoko to be granted visas included Leonard Woodcock, the president of the powerful United Auto Workers Union; the poet Allen Ginsberg; Jack Lemmon; Tony Curtis; painters Jim Dine and Roy Lichtenstein; and countless less famous supporters.

While proceeding with their legal chicanery, the government began to exert more subtle pressures. John's phone was ostentatiously tapped, exhibiting so many clicks and whirrs that he became afraid to use it. Each time he went out in the street, he was closely followed. Yet when John appeared on "The Dick Cavett Show" to tell the world what was happening to him, his fears were generally dismissed as simply the latest ravings of the balmy ex-Beatle.

In the midst of all this, John was approached by Mayor Lindsay to play a couple of benefit shows at Madison Square Garden to raise money for mentally handicapped children, to which he generously agreed. He rocked through "Hound Dog," "Come Together," "Instant Karma," and a dozen more as the audience screamed and danced on their seats.

"I was on a trip all right," he babbled afterwards. "It was just the same kind of feeling when the Beatles used to really get into it. Funnily enough, I tend to remember the times before the Beatles happened most of all. Like in Hamburg, we used to do this . . . at the Cavern, we used to do that . . . in the ballrooms, the other. In those days, we weren't just doing an entertaining thing, or whatever the hell it was we were supposed to be. That was when we played music. That's what I enjoy and remember best about those days."

Despite John's enthusiasm, the shows were the last he was ever to star in.

He produced a new album called *Mind Games,* which was interesting only for its studious avoidance of politics, and then, as the pressure of the endless court cases, the phone tapping, and being followed began to grind him down, he and Yoko moved to an apartment in a grim fortresslike New York apartment house called the Dakota. A security guard stood outside the entrance in a little security box to repel unwanted visitors twenty-four hours a day, and John began to feel less vulnerable. For a while, he had worried that whoever was trying to remove him from the United States might be tempted to resort to a more extreme course of action.

He began, suddenly, to divorce himself from the radical politics he had clutched so close a few short months previously: "That radicalism was phony really because it was born out of guilt," he said. "It was partly that and partly because I'm a chameleon. I always felt guilty that I'd made money, so I had to let people rob me in the disguise of management or whatever. I always felt that I didn't deserve it or there's something wrong with having it. It never made sense to me to have money and think the way I thought. I was always having that turmoil. The radicalism was a combination of having met certain people at certain times. So I just went along for the trip. You know, what am I doing fighting the American government just so Jerry Rubin can get a decent job?"

In the midst of everything, Yoko insisted they should both visit a specialist to see why they were unable to produce the child they both longed for. The specialist told Yoko it would be difficult for her to conceive because she had undergone more than one abortion and suffered several miscarriages. Worse still, he said that John had become infertile—apparently because of the vast quantities of drugs and alcohol which he had pumped into his bloodstream over the years. The news had visibly shaken John, making him almost as irritable and aggressive as he had been back in Liverpool. He argued furiously with Allen Klein over a business deal—and Klein promptly sued him for $200,000. John was drunk much of the time, depressed because he felt imprisoned in America: his lawyer had warned him that if he left the country for a single day, he would never be allowed back again.

As his idealistic plans and hopes deteriorated, he began to

verbally assault Yoko, tearing away at her very personality. He seemed to feel that she was responsible for the miserable mess his life had become—the failure of his music, the seemingly endless procession of court cases. Everything had seemed to go so wrong.

Yoko could feel him slipping away, knew that she was losing him. So she was unsurprised when shortly after his thirty-third birthday, John jumped on a plane to Los Angeles with May Pang, their pretty Japanese secretary.

"I went out to buy coffee and newspapers and didn't go back," he joked when friends asked him what had happened to his marriage.

With Wings, Paul now had the freedom to do all the things he would have done with the Beatles if John and George had not been so apathetic. He certainly would have loved to play small colleges to rid the Beatles of their concert nerves. Now Paul decided to revive another Fab Four idea which had misfired—*The Magical Mystery Tour*. The Wings band, he decided, would rent an open-topped, double-decker bus and set off on a crazy, funny tour of all the places he and Linda fancied visiting in Europe. They would keep each venue as secret as possible in order to keep the ever-hounding press at bay and, by the end of the tour, they would be tight enough to play proper concerts in Britain.

Besides arranging the lights, the sound system, and the order of the songs they should play, one additional small problem reared its head: where could they hide their stash of dope? When the Beatles had gone on tour, they had always carried their supply in their own hand luggage—cases which they jokingly called "diplomatic bags" because the customs men were usually too busy asking for autographs and gaping to search them. But on this tour, it would be different: they would be going through one customs post after another and, if they had the misfortune to be caught with several pounds of marijuana on them, there was every chance that they would all go to jail. They arranged, therefore, for a friend in London to mail dope to hotels where they would be staying. That way they wouldn't have to carry huge quantities around and they could always deny all knowledge of the stuff if it was intercepted by customs men.

The band's first show was at an open-air amphitheater at Château Vallon, near Toulon in the south of France. It was a jolly, sunny affair, though not remotely comparable to the bigtime aura of a Beatles' concert. Everybody seemed to be enjoying themselves. The few critics who managed to slip in to see the event were basically kind, though they were unable to say anything more generous about Linda than that she seemed to try hard.

Linda's playing seemed increasingly to be an encumrance to the rest of the band. Henry McCullough and Denny Siewell, in particular, felt that with a powerhouse keyboards player like Billy Preston, Wings was potentially a world-class band. With Linda, however, they would always be relegated to rock and roll's second division. When they began to grumble, though, Paul was very quick to silence them. In fact, they were all slightly surprised at the change which had come over Paul on this tour: where once he had been consistently charming, prepared to do anything for anyone, he was now increasingly bellicose. For the first time they could remember, he was refusing to sign autographs for over-enthusiastic fans who asked for them at inconvenient times. He also snapped and argued with hotel managers who failed to provide him with a double bed or a late meal.

"I was always very well-mannered and polite," he explained. "My dad brought me up to always tip my cap to my elders and I used to do it until I was about fourteen and I didn't wear a cap anymore. Now I force myself not to tolerate people I don't like. If people do something which irritates me, I let them know about it.

"You can so easily lose your identity in this sort of business. You confuse the myth with the person you really are. Like Marilyn Monroe must have got to the point where she didn't know who she was any more. She was a walking legend, not a person. And because she was a legend, she had to be kind and patient to every little creep who ever pestered her. I make sure that being well known doesn't stop me being an ordinary bloke who won't tolerate people he doesn't like."

After meandering slowly through France, Germany, and Switzerland, Wings arrived in Copenhagen, the capital of Denmark and one of the most liberal cities in Europe. The group visited a club there where smoking hash was permitted and they all gently puffed themselves into insensibility. The tour was going better than they had hoped—though audiences seemed slightly disappointed at Paul's stalwart refusal to play any Beatle songs. The press had become so annoyed by Paul's disinclination to talk with them that they had taken to writing scurrilous stories about Paul's arrogance and his unfriendliness.

Wings finally made headlines in August after police at Göteborg in Sweden intercepted nearly half a pound of cannabis which had been sent to Paul at the hotel from London. The drug squad was waiting backstage when Wings finished their set at the Scandinavian Hall, and Paul, Linda, and Dennis Seiwell were hauled off to the police station for questioning.

"We told them we had found marijuana in the letter and at first they said they knew nothing about it," said a police spokesman. "But after we had questioned them for about three hours, they confessed and told us the truth. McCartney, his wife, and Seiwell told us they smoked hash every day. They said they were almost addicted to it. They said they had made arrangements to have drugs posted to them every day they played in different countries so they wouldn't have to take any drugs through the customs themselves."

Fortunately for Wings, the Swedish police pride themselves on their liberal outlook on such matters. The luckless trio were freed after paying $1,000 as a surety for their future good behavior.

Among the many people who read about the case with interest were two Scotsmen—one who Paul knew well and another he had never heard of. The first was Duncan Cairns, a dour forty-one-year-old farmer who Paul paid to look after his farm while he was away. Mr. Cairns was deeply shocked by the news: to him, drugs were simply evil. In the past, friends had teased him by suggesting that his employer used drugs at High Park—but he had always defended Paul against them. Paul's drug bust was too much for him. He immediately sat down and painstakingly wrote his letter of resignation.

The second man interested in Paul's misfortune was a granite-faced character named Norman McPhee. He was particularly intrigued because he was a police constable, and at that precise moment he just happened to be in a special drugs identification course in Glasgow. Since he was based in Campbeltown, the course had seemed, at first, to be something of a waste of time—it was hard to imagine the stolid Highland crofters he protected sniffing cocaine and engaging in acid-crazed orgies. It just so happened, however, that High Park Farm was within the jurisdiction of his police station.

Within days of his return to Campbeltown, he set off for High Park, ostensibly to check that the place was secure in the absence of its illustrious owner. Why his security consciousness led him to enter Paul's greenhouse is unclear, but such was his horror at the marijuana plants he spied growing there among the tomatoes that he promptly returned to his police station for reinforcements lest, one imagines, the plants turned violent. A total of seven large-footed policemen then turned the farm over, finding absolutely nothing more of interest and Paul was eventually fined about $150.

"Well, I don't think it's as dangerous as drink," he said defiantly. "It should be like homosexuality—legal among consenting adults. I don't even think cannabis is associated with hard drugs. There is as much danger of a man who drinks ending up an alcoholic as there is of a cannabis taker graduating to hard drugs."

All this talk of drugs inspired Paul to write a song about them, "Hi, Hi, Hi"—which was, predictably enough, banned by the BBC. Fortunately, the other side of the record, "C Moon," was even better and the record became a smash hit.

When the beautiful follow-up single, "My Love," went straight to number one in the States, it was apparent that Paul had at last recovered his Beatle form.

Wings played a surprise show at London's Hard Rock Café at a party to raise funds for the drugs charity, Release—a charity that was obviously close to Paul's heart. Then Paul and Linda were off on vacation to Morocco. While they were turning mahogany in the sun and enjoying the relief of being in a land where nobody had the slightest idea who they were, a call came through from London: Sir Lew Grade, their triumphant foe in the battle for the Beatles' publishing company, Northern Songs, wanted Paul to star in a television spectacular for ATV. The program's producer flew out to discuss the details and the result was a lavish, brilliantly choreographed film called *James Paul McCartney*.

In the film, Paul interspersed hard rock like "Long Tall Sally" with a gentle solo version of "Yesterday" and lavish dancing routines. Though the show served to display vividly Paul's extraordinary versatility, it also showed just how vehement and inflexible many critics had become in their attitude toward him: "It was a showcase for Paul's amazing ability to be all things to all men, women, and little lambs," commented one writer.

Wings' new album, *Red Rose Speedway,* earned even more jeers. Paul had still failed, in his fourth attempt, to produce a really great album. Most of the music papers began to write him off as nothing more than an ex-Beatle who made occasional good singles. Their attacks on Linda were little short of libelous. She sang flat; she was an embarrassment, they reported. Paul should stop trying to turn her into a musician when it was so patently obvious that she had no talent. Mick Jagger added to the snickering when he told an interviewer that he would never let his old lady play in his band. One paper even asked, as a joke, the definition of a dog with wings. The answer was Linda McCartney.

Ironically, in recent years there had been only one celebrity's wife who had had to undergo a similar process of vilification . . . Yoko Ono.

In May of 1973, after Paul had completed the theme song for the James Bond film *Live and Let Die*, Wings set off on their first proper tour of Britain. Despite some highly insulting reviews, the tour proved to be a triumph with the audiences. Backstage, though, all was not well. Paul was becoming increasingly autocratic with Denny Seiwell and Henry McCullough—just as he had been with George and Ringo. They both began to resent the arrogant way in which he treated them as musical simpletons, forever dominating them and ordering them to play in the way he wished.

The closeness they had all enjoyed when the band started rehearsing up in Scotland, they felt, was beginning to fall apart. More and more, Paul seemed to be treating them like second-rate session musicians. McCullough and Seiwell were additionally angered by the fact that Paul seemed to listen to the ideas of Denny Laine but never to their ideas. The rows became more frequent.

Nevertheless, after three triumphant concerts at Hammersmith Odeon, things had seemed better—even Linda was beginning to play better.

When the tour ended, Paul decided that they would have to go all out to produce a really superb fifth album. If they blew it again, it seemed likely that Wings would just be written off by the music critics, whose respect Paul still craved. They would record, he decided, in Nigeria, amid the amazing rhythm sounds that Ginger Baker, Cream's former drummer, had been raving about of late. Their music would be driven in new directions and they just might be able to break free and create a completely different type of album.

During rehearsals in London a few days before they were scheduled to fly to Nigeria, Paul began to get to Henry McCullough in the same way he had gotten to George Harrison.

"Look," he snarled at one point, when a riff he wanted wasn't being played correctly. "Don't tell me it can't be played. I know it can be played."

"It's impossible," muttered Henry in retaliation. "You're wrong."

"OK—give me the guitar and I'll show you. . . ."

Henry became furious. After playing around the world with a string of bands, he wasn't prepared to be told how to play his instrument by anyone. Paul's unpleasant facility for making people feel small and worthless seemed to be causing the same discord it had in the Beatles. Wordlessly, Henry packed his guitar into its case and walked out. That evening, he phoned Paul at home to tell him he was leaving.

OK, Paul decided, we'll manage without him. But an hour before Paul's car was due to take him to the airport for the Nigerian recording session, another call came through: Denny Seiwell couldn't face working with him any longer either.

"Well, we're still going," Paul told Linda. "Even if Denny Laine decides he's quitting as well. We'll just have to make the album on our own."

"Like we did when the Beatles were breaking up?"

"Yeah."

And Linda could see the black clouds drifting back into his eyes again.

13

SOMETIMES, WHEN THE HEROIN DIDN'T COME, Eric Clapton would stub cigarettes out on his body or bang his head hard against the wall to distract himself from the sweating, dizzy, wrenching agony of withdrawal. Addiction had crept up upon him stealthily, like a cat upon a lovebird. Like most of his friends at that time, he had started out by developing a penchant for the newly fashionable drug, cocaine. Sniffing the white, crystalline dust into his nose through a rolled-up dollar bill, he had discovered, sent what felt like champagne coursing through his veins, added fire to his playing, and gave him a confidence he lacked. Everyone he knew—Rod Stewart, Mick Jagger, Keith Richards—was snorting coke, and to have declined would have been to feel like a teen-age apprentice who wishes to tell his new workmates that he doesn't like the taste of beer.

Cocaine was, of course, hardly a new drug. In the naughty 1890s, there had been a huge cocaine craze in the States as dozens of rival firms competed to market stimulating cocaine bonbons, cocaine snuff, and cocaine drinks. Sigmund Freud even believed for a spell that coke was a potent antidote to psychiatric illness and was himself a heavy user.

In 1970, the drug had been rediscovered and made fashionable once again by the rock stars and leisured aristocrats who were able to afford it. The growth in popularity of cocaine in the years which followed was an interesting reflection of the shift in attitude in the Seventies. Whereas Sixties drugs like cannabis and LSD were languorous and provided a form of escape from reality, coke's effect was a sharpening of the mind, an increasing of aggression, giving users the impression they were better equipped to cope with reality.

Eric, however, had the misfortune to purchase his supplies of cocaine from a dealer who insisted that he should also buy an equal quantity of heroin with each consignment. He had resolved to simply pop the little packets of heroin into a dusty drawer, where they silently mounted up.

But when the pain of Patti Harrison's rejection, coupled with the total commercial failure of "Layla" and all the other love songs he had written for her on his album (primarily because he released the record under the pseudonym Derek and the Dominoes) slipped him ever deeper into the abyss of depression, his resolution wavered.

One evening, he and his girlfriend had been feeling so down that they had decided that, as there was no cocaine in the house, they would try the heroin. A few seconds after he sniffed the powder, he had lost consciousness, but when he came to, moments later, he felt replete and euphoric—as though he had just eaten a wonderful meal, drunk a couple of bottles of wine, and made love.

Thereafter, the couple had snorted heroin almost every day until they were both heavily addicted.

With heroin, the actual high gradually fades away with constant usage and the addict is just left feeling constantly sleepy, constipated, impotent, and craving an ever-larger fix. Patti became just a hazy dream while she and Eric whiled away their days chasing fresh supplies of heroin, watching color television, or making models from little plastic kits. Still, though, they refused to inject themselves—even though this would have necessitated buying only one-tenth the quantity of drugs.

Eric Clapton

Eric found he was spending one hundred, then five hundred, then as much as a thousand pounds a week on the drug. At one point, when his record royalties were delayed, he sold a guitar and one of his cars to pay for supplies.

The family of Eric's girlfriend had become deeply worried and eventually they persuaded the pair of them to try a newly developed electro-acupuncture treatment, which had helped many drug addicts through withdrawal symptoms. The treatment had been developed by an attractive, dark-haired, middle-aged specialist named Dr. Meg Patterson. Dr. Patterson traveled down to Hurtwood Edge to give each of them a small electronic device and to explain how to use it. Electrodes, she said, are simply attached to their earlobes; they could then control the quantity of electricity which buzzed through their heads by adjusting a small, round dial on the console. The electric shocks would counteract the trauma of withdrawal.

Eric wasn't keen: it all sounded horrifying. He preferred to forego the treatment. But his girlfriend was insistent, and so they began the treatment the following day.

All had gone well until they began to feel the first convulsions of withdrawal. The pain, they discovered, was too great—Eric pulled off the electrodes and rushed to fetch a small packet of heroin he had hidden in a remote corner of the house. Each day, they managed to conjure up a little more. Eventually, they both realized they would never get over their addiction unless they were supervised, and they went to stay with Dr. Patterson; less than a month later, they were cured.

Eric decided that, unless he completely cut himself off from the rock world, he would probably become addicted again; and so, as spring brightened the sodden fields with daffodils and almond blossoms, he kissed his friend farewell and set off for Wales to dig and sweat on a friend's farm. The hard labor cleared his head and steeled his resolve: he knew exactly what he had to do. He wasn't even nervous when he dialed the telephone number he had known by heart for so many years. "Hello, Patti," he said. "It's me . . ."

George had planned to play a concert for 100,000 people at London's Wembley Stadium as a follow-up to his show at Madison Square Garden. The money from this event, he intended, would also be given to the starving children of Bangladesh. Perhaps, he said, he would go so far as to play more concerts in other major cities around the world. The Internal Revenue Service, however, when they discovered that profits from the spin-offs after the Madison Square Garden show were expected to amount to nearly $20 million, effectively froze most of the money for several years while determining how much they could clutch into their coffers— a delay which may have resulted in the needless death of many thousands of starving people in East Pakistan. George, justifiably angry, launched a bitter tirade against the money men when he was interviewed by Dick Cavett for his American TV show.

But he remained spectacularly generous to anyone who came to him with a reasonable claim on his fortune. And when Allan Williams, the Beatles' diminutive first manager, showed up at Apple slightly the worse for wear and swearing profusely, George proved to be generous again.

Williams wanted George to pay him a few thousand pounds for a rough tape which had been recorded when the Beatles were playing at a club in Hamburg twelve years before. He felt the Beatles owed him something for the help he had given them at the start of their career. Ringo had already refused to give him money but George, listening patiently, agreed that Williams had given them all a helping shove on their way. Telling the former manager to hold out his hands, George poured a sack of small objects into them.

At first, Williams thought it was a joke—he thought he'd been given a handful of peanuts. But then George told him he was holding sixteen uncut rubies. It was an entirely typical gesture.

Sadly, despite his generosity and deep spirituality, George was becoming increasingly unhappy: after six years of marriage, he still had no children and Patti was becoming increasingly bored with her isolated, lonely life at Friar Park. She wanted to go back to modeling or acting, but George was not keen on it. He hated the thought of all the publicity that would result if Patti were to begin working again.

By the autumn of 1972, they were arguing so much that George simply jumped into his new BMW car and set off for the Mediterranean to think things over. He stayed with his friend, singer Gary Wright, at his villa at Albufeira in Portugal. When he returned home, however, he and Patti had made up.

His deepening depression glowered through his next album, *Living in the Material World*. Harrison, in an album of offensive self-righteousness, sang of his own goodness and godliness while clumsily dismissing lesser mortals, rather in the fashion of a hellfire-and-brimstone Victorian preacher. Nevertheless, the record yielded an excellent single, "Give

Me Love (Give Me Peace on Earth)," and it sold well.

His success had cheered him but little, however, as his marriage continued to disintegrate. His dreams of filling Friar Park with the sound of children's laughter—just as it had been in Sir Frank Crisp's day—seemed to be vanishing like mist on a summer's morn.

Toward the end of 1973, Patti enjoyed a brief fling with Ronnie Wood, who was subsequently to become a member of the Rolling Stones, at his perfect Georgian mansion overlooking Richmond Hill. Then, defying George, she agreed to model at a fashion show for Ossie Clark in Chelsea.

George fled to India, where he meditated and talked with holy men for weeks on end. He returned full of enthusiasm: he would go back on the road, he and Patti could make a go of their lives. But it was already too late. Patti left him to stay with her sister, Jenny, and Jenny's husband, Mick Fleetwood of Fleetwood Mac, at their home in Los Angeles.

Eric Clapton had gone to Miami to record his comeback album, *461 Ocean Boulevard,* and then he had set off on a tour of the States. Patti flew out to join him and fell deeply and passionately in love: Layla and Majnun were together at last. For Eric, the heroin and the agony were gone, and from now on he was determined to spend his days writing and singing songs about his and Patti's perfect love.

George stoically realized that if she had to go off with someone, better Eric than anyone else. He had consoled himself by phoning up Kathy Simmonds, a frothy twenty-four-year-old blonde who had once lived with Rod Stewart. After a few steamy nights together, the two of them slipped away to Grenada in the West Indies where he taught her about meditation and vegetarian cookery in between their sessions of lolling in the sun and making torrid love.

When a reporter tracked them down to their isolated villa, George, clad only in a sarong, talked openly about the breakdown of his marriage.

"It's no big deal," he said. "We've been separated many times, but this time I don't know what will happen. I last talked to Patti in June when she left for Los Angeles to spend some time with her sister. I understand she is now with Eric Clapton. Eric is a fantastic guy. He's always been a close friend of mine—you always hurt the one you love.

"We were getting on each other's nerves and, what with the pace of my work, splitting up was the easiest thing to do. In this life, there is no time to lose in an uncomfortable situation."

On their return, Kathy had bubbled with love for George: she became a strict vegetarian, gave away her leather shoes and fur coats, ploughed through unintelligible books on the subject of Krishna consciousness—but all to no avail. George flew off to a house he had purchased in Los Angeles to finalize plans for his first concert tour since the days of Beatlemania eight years before. Their affair was over.

In the following weeks, George continued to make light of the breakdown of his marriage. At one press conference, he said: "I'm pleased about it. He's an old friend of mine and I would rather have her going out with someone like him than some other dope."

But privately he was torn in two, confused, battered, and lost. Frequently, he would obliterate reality with huge tumblers of brandy, directly contradicting the dictates of his religion.

When George arrived in the States he was taken aback by the huge buildup his tour had received. None of the other Beatles had toured America and a huge wave of nostalgia for the heady days of Beatlemania was washing over the country. Newspapers and magazines carried articles about the Beatles and the film of George's Bangladesh concert continued to fill cinemas.

Yet when George finally agreed to meet the press in Los Angeles just before the start of the tour, he was wan, exhausted-looking, and keen only to smash the beloved Beatle myth apart.

"Having played with other musicians I don't even think the Beatles were that good," he said. "It's all a fantasy, this idea of putting the Beatles back together again. The only way it will happen is if we're all broke. Even then I wouldn't relish playing with Paul. He's a fine bass player but he's sometimes overpowering. Ringo's got the best backbeat in the business—I'd join a band with John Lennon any day. But I wouldn't join a band with Paul McCartney. That's not personal; it's from a musician's point of view. Anyway, we're all enjoying being individuals. We'd all been boxed in for ten years. The biggest break in my career was getting in the Beatles in 1963. The second biggest break since then is getting out of them."

Despite his sacrilege, a roar of welcome and excitement rose from the crowd when George strolled onto the stage in front of the twenty-two predominantly Indian musicians who made up his backing orchestra for this tour. For many people, simply seeing a Beatle in the flesh was cause for jubilation.

However, even the most fervent of George's fans were taken aback by his thin, whiny voice and by the unrelieved gloom of the show. "I want you all to chant 'Hare, Hare!'" he told them at one point. When the audience's response was less than ecstatic, George began to berate them as though they were a class of naughty schoolchildren: "I don't know what you think," he snarled at them after a few seconds, "but from up here you sound pretty dead."

At another gig, he snapped petulantly: "I'd just like to tell you the Lord is in your hearts. I'm not up here jumping like a looney for my own sake but to tell you that the Lord is in your hearts. Somebody's got to tell you. Let us reflect him in one another."

Even Beatle songs were wrecked by George's misguided piety. John's delightful "In My Life," for example, had the lyrics changed so that it became yet another dreary hymn to God.

"I know we get ten people who say the show sucks every night," George complained. "And we get a hundred who, when we ask them did they like the show, say: 'We got much more than we ever hoped for.' I don't care if nobody comes to see me, nobody ever buys another record of me. I don't give a shit, it doesn't matter to me, but I'm going to do what I feel within myself. Gandhi says create and preserve the image of your choice. The image of my choice is not Beatle George. But why live in the past? Be here now, and now, whether you like me or not, is where I am.

"Fuck, my life belongs to me. It actually doesn't. It belongs to Him. My life belongs to the Lord Krishna and there's me dog collar to prove it. I'm just a dog and I'm led around by me dog collar by Krishna. I'm just the servant of the servant of the servant of the servant of Krishna. That's how I feel. Never been so humble in all my life and I feel great."

As the critics hurled their most derogatory adjectives, George's gathering gloom was relieved momentarily when Jack Ford, President Ford's son, invited him to the White House for lunch on the day he was to play Washington. President Ford, who was no slouch at garnering publicity, allowed himself to be photographed with the ex-Beatle, then mumbled his excuses and fled before George could explain his theosophical theories to him.

After the tour, George slipped into a deep depression, a state which was not relieved when he saw his new album, *Dark Horse,* destroyed by critics and ignored by record buyers. The LP was memorable only for George's acidic attack on Eric and Patti in a distorted version of the old Everly Brothers hit, "Bye Bye Love."

George's lawyers were preparing for a plagiarism case over "My Sweet Lord." They felt it unlikely, they cautioned, that George would win.

George began to withdraw from society, shunning company, rarely going out. When he became severely, frighteningly ill with a liver complaint, it began to seem as though George had lost his will to live.

Many of his friends began to fear that he would not recover.

14

1973 MARKED THE YEAR THE United States, the mightiest, most technologically advanced nation on earth, after twelve years, 56,000 American lives and millions of tons of napalm, rockets, cannon shells, chemical defoliants, and just about every other ghastly device known to mankind, withdrew in ignominious defeat at the hands of a decimated peasant army.

At a time when America was still reeling from this body-blow, the lifting of the grubby petticoats of President Nixon's administration exposed the squalid scandal that was to become known as Watergate, the affair which would eventually lead to President Nixon's resignation.

But neither of these sordid events was destined to profoundly change life for everyone in the West as greatly as the seemingly inconsequential Yom Kippur war, which flared between Israel and her Arab enemies in October. In direct consequence of the West's support for Israel, the Arab sheikhs were to literally quadruple the price of their oil in the year that followed, thus throwing the West into financial confusion and chaos, and a deep recession. The repercussions of that small war were to be felt through the rest of the decade.

In Britain, as Edward Heath's inept handling of the trade unions began to precipitate an all-out war of black-outs, three-day weeks, and fury, there was even wild talk of revolution and right-wing coups.

It was small wonder, therefore, that many people were beginning to look back nostalgically at the halcyon days of the Sixties. For many people, that halcyon existence was represented by the Beatles. If somehow the Beatles were reunited, it was vaguely felt, all would be right with the world.

Journalists, ever eager to give their readers what they wanted, sprinkled stories of gloom and despondency with such headlines as "BEATLES WILL GET TOGETHER AGAIN— EXCLUSIVE," or "WE CAN WORK IT OUT, SAYS PAUL."

The stories, as it turned out, were not as far removed from the truth as some people believed. Now that they had finally managed to empty their heads of all their solo projects, the Beatles were in a conciliatory mood.

Amidst conditions of stringent secrecy, the four of them did, in fact, spend part of 1973 working on a joint project. The reasons for their reunion were twofold: first, they had, on March 31, finally terminated their ties with Allen Klein (though there was still to be a long series of legal squabbles which eventually would result in Klein receiving something over $5 million for his services). And second, they all felt it was time they did something to put Ringo back on his feet. Following his first two flops, Ringo had not dared to put out an album for the next three years—though George had helped him to have a couple of big hit singles with his productions of "It Don't Come Easy" and "Back Off Boogaloo."

But now the three of them felt it was incumbent upon them to give him a really successful album. John had started the ball rolling by writing a lovely, jangley, Beatley song called "I'm the Greatest." On the night they were to record it John, Ringo, and their old friend, Klaus Voorman, were all sitting in the studio ready to go when George Harrison called.

"I hear there's some recording going on," he told Richard Perry, Ringo's startled producer. "Can I come down?"

"Is it okay?" Perry asked John nervously, his hand clamped tightly over the telephone's mouthpiece.

"Hell, yes," said Lennon. "Tell him to get right down here and help me finish this bridge."

"George arrived," Perry recalls. "And, without saying a word, he joined in on the same wavelength we were on. He played guitar and John played piano, and they complemented each other perfectly. There was the Beatles' magic unfolding right before my eyes."

Paul had wanted to fly out to the States to join in with the session but he had been refused a visa because of his conviction for growing marijuana. So he had contented himself by writing a song called "Six O'Clock," which he played and sang on when Ringo returned to London.

George wrote two tracks: "Photograph," which subsequently became a hit single, and "Sunshine Life for Me."

After the inconsistency of their solo careers and the problems of playing with new musicians, they had all enjoyed being together again.

"I really like the album," John said, when it was over. "And I really enjoyed working with George and Ringo again. Unfortunately, Paul could not come out to the States to work on the record because he could not get a visa. But I think that we will play together again."

Paul, too, enjoyed the experience: "Yes, we will work together again," he said. "I think that we will just meet and decide to do one or two things together, and it will grow from there. There is no hurry. We split in 1970 because we all grew up. When we split, it was like getting out of the army for all of us. We always said we would not stagger on until we were ninety, and I think the split finally came because the Beatles, as they were then, had come to an end.

"Even now I can't ever see us walking out onto a stage again and singing our old numbers. But there are other things we can do together—and we will."

At first, Ringo's career had seemed to dead-end without the Beatles. He had spent most of his days plodding lugubriously around the garden of his Highgate house wondering what he possibly could find now to occupy his days. But then, quite suddenly, once he had got over the shock and the unpleasantness of the break-up, he had hurled himself into a frenzy of activity. He had taken guitar lessons, hoping that he would eventually be able to start seriously composing songs.

That particular venture led nowhere. But a chance meeting with a young, bright furniture designer named Robin Cruikshank was to prove considerably more fruitful. As they talked, Cruikshank became immediately aware that Ringo had a natural passion for Art Deco and that he was a font of ideas for new furniture designs in sympathy with this fashionable 1930s style.

Ringo told him that he liked the idea of building a coffee table around two Rolls-Royce radiator grilles. It was, Cruikshank thought, an outrageous idea—but possibly also a very commercial one. Ringo also wanted to produce a geometric, free-standing mirror with an Apple logo in the center. At their next meeting, the two of them had sketched out some of their ideas—wonderful circular fireplaces, tables shaped like flowers—and they had decided they would have to have some of their ideas made up.

Robin contacted some friendly furniture manufacturers and, once they had seen the imaginative results, the two of them decided to set up a proper company, which they called Ringo Or Robin, Ltd.

As they only made a few pieces of furniture from each design, their furniture was terrifyingly expensive: a small mirror cost $100, a sofa $1500. But, to their surprise, they found they could not produce their furniture fast enough to satisfy demand. Among their most enthusiastic patrons was the prime minister, Edward Heath, who took time off from battling with striking workers to scatter his private apartment at 10 Downing Street with Ringo's and Robin's creations of stainless steel-and-glass.

Ringo in a London pub with an unidentified friend

To show their appreciation, Ringo presented the premier with a specially designed mirror for Christmas in 1973. The mirror showed Mr. Heath facing his own reflection over a pastoral English landscape. Appropriately, for a man who was driving inexorably toward confrontation with British miners, a few black clouds floated overhead.

When Ringo heard of a new band named T. Rex, which was beginning to take Britain by storm, he watched the excitement, heard the adoring chatter of his own small children, and felt bemused and slightly old. On a whim, he phoned Marc Bolan, the band leader, to suggest he should come to see him. They could, he thought, use Apple Films to make a movie of T. Rex in concert. As they talked, Ringo became increasingly taken by Bolan's open charm, his zany humor, and his very genuine sense of astonishment at all that had happened to him. Immediately, the two of them became close friends, drinking and looning together all over London.

"He is almost like a father to me," Marc said. "He has been through it all before and there's so much he has taught me that it would have taken me a lot of years and a lot of pain to learn on my own."

At one point, the two of them went on a vacation together to Barbados, together with Marc's wife, June. Maureen had stayed at home to look after the children—she hadn't thought it was right to take them away from school and, besides, she hated the sun.

As soon as the three of them took their seats on the plane, they had been served free champagne which they gulped down at astonishing speed so that within an hour they were all hysterically, wonderfully drunk. They put on headsets to watch the in-flight movie, a comedy, and they had screamed until tears ran down their faces at every mildly amusing incident.

Early on in the flight, a crotchety fellow passenger, apoplectic with rage at their raucous behavior, bonked them on the head with his paperback book, tore off their headsets, and called the chief steward.

When the steward tried to remonstrate, Ringo and Marc had made faces until he collapsed into a seat beside Ringo, doubled over with laughter. The complaining passengers too had become infected with the giggles and, from there on, the entire first-class compartment was laughing and drinking its way to the West Indies.

The holiday was, unfortunately, less successful. Ringo had

never tried sunbathing anywhere so hot before and, after the first day, he was convulsed in an agony of sunburn. From then on, taking no chances, he had spent every day hidden behind a hat, a cardboard nose-protector, sunglasses, jeans, and a long-sleeved T-shirt. When he returned home, Maureen was amazed to find he was still almost as pale as he had been when he left.

The holiday did have a serious side, however: it was the first time Ringo had ever gone on vacation without Maureen. The strain of spending weeks on end together following the demise of the Beatles was beginning to put a strain on their relationship.

Ringo next decided to play at being a film director, putting together a movie based around a huge concert T. Rex was playing at Wembley. Elton John joined in and the three of them turned the venture into a slightly surreal extravaganza, with Ringo dressing as a bear and dancing about with Marc for some of the loopier scenes. The result was entitled *Born to Boogie*, and though the critics didn't like it, they weren't really meant to. For thousands of Marc's adoring fans, the film was a work of genius.

Ringo's growing stature as an actor, however, was unquestioned. After *Candy* and *The Magic Christian* and the western, *Blindman,* he acted the part of a Liverpool teddy-boy in Ray Connolly's brilliantly recorded film about Fifties' teen-age life, *That'll Be the Day.* His performance earned rave reviews and most critics agreed that he stole the show.

In an effort to hold their marriage together, Ringo and Maureen had bought John's house, Tittenhurst Park. It proved to be an unwise change, for Ringo and Maureen had become as disoriented and lost among the seventy-four acres of parkland, the Tudor tea cottage, the four staff cottages, the swimming pool, the recording studio, the tennis courts, and the eight-bedroom, four-bathroom, four-reception room mansion as John and Yoko had been. John and Yoko's terrified reaction to this sterile grandeur had been to flee to a two-room apartment in the heart of New York. Ringo and Maureen's response was to drink and to fight.

Ringo also seemed to become more volatile and full of self-importance. He was lord of the manor now and he wanted very much to be taken seriously; the years of being lovable, cuddly, soppy Ringo were over, and woe betide the person who failed to realize it. One girl who used to work with him at this time remembered that he would occasionally give verbal tongue-lashings that would leave her weeping.

His friendship with Billy Smart, the owner of the nearby Windsor Safari Park, fell apart over a fairly trivial incident. On the evening Smart invited Ringo and Maureen to attend the opening of a new nightclub at the park, Ringo walked through the door and immediately spotted a photographer carelessly loitering at the bar. Ignoring greetings from friends, Ringo marched across the crowded room, tapped the photographer on the shoulder, and told the startled man: "If you take my picture, mate, I'll stick one on you." The disillusioned cameraman scampered back to his newspaper and Ringo pronounced icily that his friendship with Billy Smart was at an end.

The drinking bouts at Tittenhurst Park became increasingly wild and they occasionally ended with bets as to who could drive the twenty-five miles to the nightclub Tramp, in London's West End, the fastest. Ringo usually managed to complete the journey in his Mercedes in less than half an hour. On one occasion, he was going so fast that he skidded off the road into a ditch and ricocheted off a tree back into the road again. He carried on with the hell-for-leather race with barely a pause.

Although he had a chauffeur, Ringo invariably felt like driving himself once he had downed a few drinks. Very often, he would come out of a nightclub and simply tell his chauffeur to move over so he could drive. On one occasion, the police stopped him in the early hours of the morning, after a hard night at Tramp. But he had simply smiled

Ringo's wife Maureen

winningly, charmed the policemen, and ended up signing autographs for the policemen's children.

Everywhere he went he was surrounded by beautiful girls who found his charm, his fame, and his wealth an irresistible combination. Maureen became increasingly unhappy. In her efforts to please him, she would dye her hair blonde, dark, or wear it in tumbling curls.

"It seemed," says one friend, "that he needed to attract these girls to rid himself of his feelings of insecurity. He had been labeled for so long as the least significant member of the Beatles that he was desperate to assert himself, if only by attracting beautiful girls."

Maureen wasn't equipped to cope with this kind of competition. She had been just sixteen, a junior assistant in a hairdresser's shop, when Ringo had plucked her out of the crowd of pretty kids who swarmed around the Beatles at the Cavern in Liverpool. They married two years later and their first son was born the same year. Now she had three children and she worried about losing her looks. Desperately, she began to gulp down slimming tablets so she could become as greyhound-lean as the leggy models who scampered after her husband.

Unfortunately, the pills seemed to make her twitchy, edgy, and she and Ringo argued constantly; one day he finally walked out, slamming the door, and jumped on a plane to Los Angeles—never to return.

George and Patti Harrison in July of 1972

"I was married and I had a wonderful marriage," says Ringo stoically. "For me, it was for life when we started. But then it comes to the point where it didn't work. So, you know, and you try all these different rooms, and: 'Let's do it for the children,' and all that bullshit and, in the end, you have to look at it here and say: 'It's not working anyway.'

"Why am I staying here? Why am I doing this? Why is she into that? She's probably into that because I'm into this, and then it's the breakdown. And I'm northern, so once it's broken, I cut it off as fast as I can. It's just an attitude I have: once it's gone, it's gone. . . ."

Maureen divorced him in July, 1975, on the grounds of his admitted adultery with an American actress named Nancy Andrews.

15

ONE DAY IN LAGOS while recording his new album, Paul found he could hardly breathe: he gasped desperately for air like a netted fish, before staggering from the fetid atmosphere of the recording studio out into the dusty, noisy African street. Still he could not breathe. It was as though a pillow was being held over his face by some invisible hand. A terrible, searing pain ripped through the right side of his chest and he could feel himself trembling.

"I'm going to die," he thought hazily. He knew people of his age, thirty-one, could have heart attacks, of course. But he had never dreamed it might happen to him. Slowly, the world drifted out of focus.

"Don't worry," the doctor told him when he floated back into consciousness. "All you need is a few days in bed. It's nothing serious."

Paul remained convinced that death was imminent for several days, but then he had started to feel stronger and, before long, he was back in the studio again.

Denny Laine *had* turned up to record with him and Linda in Lagos. But the desertion of Denny Seiwell and Henry McCullough had recalled the awful specters of the Beatle break-up, and had left Paul with the same unpleasant feelings of guilt he had experienced when George Harrison

191

had complained that he couldn't bear to work with him anymore.

His confusion was made greater by the reality of Lagos: instead of the idyllic tropical paradise he had hoped for, he found a steamy, stinking city of broken shacks and hostile countrymen. One evening, as he and Linda strolled through a quiet corner of the city to visit the house where Denny was staying, a gang of five men began following them in a battered, dusty old car. Paul assumed that, even in this far corner of the earth, he had been recognized: it seemed there was nowhere left on earth where he could walk without being pestered by fans. But these men were no curious admirers: they suddenly burst from the car with long-bladed knives—gesticulating frantically—demanded money, cameras, and watches.

"Don't kill us," Linda screamed. "We're musicians—he's Beatle Paul—don't kill him."

One of the men laughed contemptuously, then they grabbed their loot, slipped back into the car, and vanished into the night.

The policeman smiled when they told him what had happened: "You're very lucky," he said. "If you'd been black, they would have killed you. But they know that you won't identify them because to white folks all us blacks look alike."

One night, at the urging of Cream's former drummer Ginger Baker, who now lived in Lagos, they had all gone to a sweaty club owned by a Nigerian musician called Fela Ransome-Kuti. When they arrived, Ransome-Kuti was onstage playing an exhilarating throbbing music replete with the power and mystery of a jungle river. Paul, rocking up and down to the rhythm, relaxed for the first time in weeks, suddenly happy again. Tears of joy were pouring down his face in an unstoppable stream. The magical evening had ended unpleasantly, however. Ransome-Kuti, who had been offish at first, accused Paul of only coming to Lagos to steal black music, to exploit Nigerian musicians for his own gain. He should get back to England where he came from.

"Look, we've done all right without Africa so far," Paul remonstrated. "Nobody's going to swipe your music." An uneasy friendship developed between the two men, though Paul felt compelled thereafter to studiously avoid the temptation to make any of his songs sound remotely Nigerian.

Paul knew that to a large degree his reputation rested on the record he was recording in Lagos. After four heavily criticized LPs, he had to pull something wonderful out of the bag this time, something comparable to John Lennon's beautiful *Imagine* album.

Miraculously, *Band on the Run,* tempered by the misery and stress Paul endured during its recording, was not merely good—it was a work of shimmering brilliance, better, in many ways, than several of the Beatles' albums. It jumped straight to the top of the charts in almost every country in the world, selling more than six million copies, yielding three hit singles, and forcing Paul's most vehement critics to eat every one of their harsh words.

In gratitude to Denny Laine's loyalty, Paul had signed over a share of the royalties from *Band on the Run* to him—a share which proved so huge that it enabled Denny to move overnight from a humble houseboat on the Thames to a stately mansion.

Despite the success of *Band on the Run,* Paul knew that he needed some new musicians if he was to tour again. Besides, he never again wanted to go through the trauma of making an album under the kind of pressures he'd endured in Lagos.

The two musicians he recruited could not have been more different from one another. Geoff Britton was a tall, blond, easygoing Cockney drummer who enjoyed karate and came from a band called East of Eden. Jimmy McCullough was a tiny, dark-haired Glaswegian who drank like a sailor on leave, swore like a truckdriver, and played guitar like an angel. Of the two, McCullough was by far the more interesting: though only twenty-one years old, his playing had a sufficient hint of genius to lead to frequent comparisons with Eric Clapton. The Who's Pete Townshend had been so impressed by his skills that he had helped McCullough's band, Thunderclap Newman, to have a huge hit with the song "Something in the Air." And Jimmy, who was just sixteen, had followed up with gigs with two hugely respected bands—John Mayall's Blues-breakers and Stone the Crow.

Though Paul had been impressed by the playing of both McCullough and Britton, the two loathed one another from their first meeting. McCullough, who had been drinking, viciously criticized the new drummer's playing.

"I hated his guts," retaliated Britton, simply.

By the time the band had cut three tracks for Wings' follow-up album to *Band on the Run,* the situation had become intolerable, and Geoff Britton found himself leaving Wings as suddenly as he had joined. He was rapidly replaced by Joe English, who had until then been playing with Delaney and Bonnie. As he was Wings' third drummer in as many years, the rock world had not been exactly shaken to its foundations by his arrival.

Paul recorded most of the new album, which was to be entitled *Venus and Mars,* in New Orleans, a city famed for the potency of the marijuana available there. Certainly, Paul and Linda had had no complaints.

Their indulgence soon led to misfortune, however. When Paul, sharing a joint with Linda, inadvertently drove through a red light in Los Angeles, a highway patrol motorcyclist immediately flagged them down. Though they threw the joint they were puffing to the floor, the policeman smelled its heady aroma and immediately leaned into the car as the McCartneys' three children looked on nervously from the back seat.

After discovering the still-smoldering joint, he searched them both until he found Linda's small stash of marijuana in her handbag. Paul was mortified: he had been refused a visa to enter the U.S. for years because of that silly conviction for growing marijuana on his farm. Now he would, in all probability, be deported.

"It's all mine," Linda butted in hastily. "It's nothing at all to do with him."

Fortunately, the patrolman accepted her story and seemed content to charge her alone. Eventually, a court in Los Angeles told Linda that if she spent six sessions with a psychiatrist who would tell her how awful drugs were, the charges would be dropped. Linda had gaily agreed to take part in the farce and, eventually, the case was dismissed.

In April of 1975, after Apple had been disbanded, Badfinger, the band Paul had launched by writing their first hit "Come and Get It," had been tumbled into disarray. Despite more hits, Pete Ham, their leader, had been left confused and lost without Paul's paternal guidance. Because of the chaos into which his affairs had been thrown after Apple's demise, at age twenty-seven he was broke. To make matters worse, his girlfriend, Ann Ferguson, was expecting their second child, he was $1200 overdrawn at the bank and there was no way he could afford to pay the mortgage on his new $50,000 house at Woking in Surrey. After a long talk with Badfinger's bass player, Tom Evans, he returned home one April evening, gulped down a few drinks, and walked calmly out to his garage and hanged himself.

Paul was still in Los Angeles when he heard the news. "It upset me because he was so good," he said. "It was one of those horrible things where you think what if. . . ? What if I had called him a week ago? Would that maybe have stopped him doing it? You always wonder."

As with every upset, minor and major, Paul responded by throwing himself even more deeply into his work. *Venus and Mars,* the long-awaited follow-up to *Band on the Run,* was finally unleashed on the world in the summer of 1975. It would have been superb except that Paul—with the same extraordinary lack of judgment which persuaded him to release "Mary Had a Little Lamb" as a single—included a mammoth interpretation of the theme from "Crossroads," Britain's wettest, dreariest television soap opera, on one side of the record.

Despite this *faux pas,* the record sold by the millions around the world, and it finally gave Paul the confidence to take Wings' new lineup on a major tour, earning him rave reviews in Britain and Australia.

The climax of the tour was to be a series of concerts in Japan—where Wings were so popular that they were selling more records than they were in any country in Europe, including Britain.

Arrangements were made with Japanese promoters, concert halls were booked, flights were arranged, tickets sold, and the whole band had their visas stamped into their passports by the Japanese embassy in London in preparation for the trip.

Then, as the Wings band members packed their luggage for the flight to Tokyo from Australia, a message came through for Paul from the minister of justice in Japan: Paul's visa was being canceled because of his drug conviction. The band had all been upset, especially Denny, who had been looking forward to visiting Japan for many years.

To console their Japanese fans, Paul arranged for a film of one of their triumphant Australian concerts to be screened on Japanese television. At first, the Japanese broadcasters had been less than enthusiastic—they feared that screening the film might be seen by some as an endorsement for McCartney's immoral and much-publicized drug use. But, after much soul-searching and debate, they decided to air the film, which they then tied to a long televised debate on the evils of marijuana.

Paul was less than ecstatic: "In a way, we've become martyrs for the cause," he said. "And that's a drag. . . ."

But Paul was only momentarily demoralized. Soon he was hard at work recording a new album, *Wings at the Speed of Sound.* The LP included one of Paul's most personal songs, "Let 'em In," in which Paul sings about some of the people he loves most: his Uncle Albert, brother Michael and Auntie Gin. In an effort to make Wings more of a band and less of a backing group, Paul encouraged the rest of the band to sing and write songs for the record, as well.

Paul's song about members of his family signaled an increasing dependence on his family that had begun after the break-up of the Beatles. He and Linda bought a house in Liverpool, and they tried never to miss family weddings and celebrations. His years of superstardom had given him a

Paul and Linda eating on the run, London

healthy mistrust for outsiders and, though outwardly charming, virtually no one outside his immediate family was
allowed to come too close. He even treated the people who
worked for him, with the sole exception of Denny Laine, with
a certain disdain—consequently, there tended to be a high
turnover rate among his office staff.

The wizened, old Chinese acupuncturist leaned back in
his chair and there was a smile in his dark eyes as he looked
first at John, then at Yoko.

"You behave yourself," he said quietly. "No drugs, eat well,
no drink. You have child in eighteen months."

Yoko had begun to protest: she was forty-two years old.
Other doctors had said she and John could not possibly
produce a baby—she had had too many miscarriages
and abortions, there was something wrong with John's
sperm. . . .

She also remembered her last pregnancy, back in the
Sixties, when she suffered complications. Doctors had ordered her to be confined to bed at Queen Charlotte's
Maternity Hospital. John had been distraught: he had already recorded the child's fetal heartbeat and he was con-
sumed with excitement at the thought of Yoko producing his
child. Desperately, he had arranged for the hospital to allow
him to sleep on the floor beside Yoko's bed in an old sleeping
bag. Later, the hospital's nurses had taken pity on him and
had given him a spare bed to lie in. He and Yoko had felt so
close that they seemed to be going through the same pain.

When, on November 21, she lost the child, they both cried
themselves to sleep.

"Forget what the other doctors said," the acupuncturist
interrupted firmly. "You have child."

It was January of 1975 and, though John and Yoko had
grown close again, they were still living apart. John continued to share a flat in Greenwich Village with May Pang.
But he and Yoko knew it was almost over, that they would

soon be together. Less than a week later, Yoko asked John to visit a friend of hers who was a hypnotist. He would help John to give up smoking.

After John did as she requested, he returned at last to Yoko, never to leave again.

"I feel I've been on Sinbad's voyage," he said. "I've beaten all the monsters and now, at last, I've come home."

It was more than a year since he had fled from the Dakota to Los Angeles with May, running from his and Yoko's bitter arguments, the persecution of the Immigration Department, the onset of middle age, the failure of his records, Kyoko's custody case . . . everything . . . and everyone.

Creatively, his intention had been to return to his musical roots, the gritty rock 'n' roll music he had loved before all the flower power and the bagism and the peace politics. And he knew there was no better person to take him back there than Phil Spector. Spector shared with John a mad passion for crude, thundering, mountainous rock music. But when John had called to see him at his heavily guarded mansion on Sunset Strip, Spector had not been enthusiastic. The last time John had asked his help, during the recording of *Imagine,* he had not been given a free hand. John had dominated him, used him as little more than a studio technician.

"No, no," John reassured him. "I want you to just use me as a session singer. Get me doing whatever you want just like I was part of the Crystals or the Ronettes or someone. Do whatever you like and I'll just listen to the finished take. . . ."

Still Spector had been wary. But after more than a month, John had worn down his resistance and they had started work together in the studio. It had started off wonderfully: Spector brought in thirty or more musicians at a time to back up John while he sang, gradually building up the legendary Spector "wall-of-sound." John had been thrilled. He had always been impressed by Spector-produced singles, such as "River Deep, Mountain High" and "You've Lost That Lovin' Feelin'."

Spector, too, was surfing along with a wave of excitement, high on the joy of being unleashed, and able to overindulge himself once again.

Spector's manic behavior, his wild eccentricity, was well known throughout the world of rock. So John was not too astonished when Spector began arriving at the studio with a gun, although once there was an enormously loud bang from the direction of the Record Plant's lavatory. Spector also took to knocking back ever-increasing quantities of brandy with John and any of the other musicians who happened to be around. John liked booze—it blotted out the turmoil inside his mind, stopped him from thinking too much. But then Phil began to miss sessions, and on the days he did arrive, John was often so smashed that he could barely sing.

Suddenly, Spector retreated from the world into his huge mansion and when John tried to see him, he was turned away by burly security guards.

"He's been in a motorcycle crash," he was told. Or later: "He's ill, he's dying. . . ."

John became lost, confused. He had been relying on this album to pull the threads of his life together, and now even this project had turned into chaos. His bafflement only increased when he discovered that Spector had arranged for Warner's to pay for the recording session, despite the fact that John was signed to Capitol. Even if Spector did return to the land of the living, it looked as though there would almost certainly be lawsuits.

He couldn't go home to Yoko in New York. He somehow had to persuade Spector to hand over the tapes they had recorded together. Any day now, he thought, he would be deported and then he'd never see the tapes again. While he waited, he drank ever more brandy. May Pang had no control over him; he treated her exactly as he had treated his first wife, Cynthia—fondly, but with little respect.

He began visiting bars and clubs with his old friend, singer Harry Nilsson. One night they both arrived very drunk at the Troubadour Club, where the Smothers Brothers were performing. Several journalists whom John knew had come to see the show, but John and Harry were too far gone even to notice them.

They both began heckling the performance as they downed one Brandy Alexander after another. At first, the audience was amused, but John and Harry's slurred and drunken insults rapidly became boring. Eventually, John staggered shakily to the lavatory to return with a sanitary towel plastered to his forehead. He had, he said, seen the towel-dispensing machine and it seemed a good idea at the time.

Harry had roared with laughter but the long-suffering waitress had been less amused. They had, she told them, drunk quite enough for one evening.

"Do you know who I am?" John remonstrated noisily.

"Yes," she replied looking straight into his lidded eyes, "you're an asshole with a Kotex on."

Moments later, John and Harry were physically ejected from the club. When a girl photographer had started snapping photographs of the debacle, John had lunged violently toward her, filled once again with all the anger which had made him a feared streetfighter in Liverpool.

The following morning, the story and the photographs appeared in newspapers in almost every country in the world.

"I think," John said to Harry, "we should maybe get down to some work while we are waiting for Phil to come back. Why don't I produce an album for you?"

They had rented a huge mansion on Pacific Coast Highway, a vast palace where both Marilyn Monroe and Peter Lawford had once lived. Then they invited all the best musicians they could think of—Ringo, Klaus Voorman, Keith Moon, and Bobby Keyes—to stay with them while they worked on the record. Once the record companies heard that John was working with Harry, they were falling over one another to dole out huge advances, regardless of what kind of album it was going to be.

For the album, John decided that Harry should do exactly what John himself had been trying to do with Phil Spector—put some new life into great, old rock 'n' roll classics. The record would be called *Pussycats,* though nobody quite knew why.

Somehow, though, they couldn't seem to actually begin work. They would all start drinking vodka when they woke up in the early afternoon, then gradually move on to brandy as midnight approached. They invented wonderful games, such as daring one another to leap from moving cars. In addition to their drinking, they were now all dropping Librium, Valium, and any other pills they could lay their hands on.

"My goal was to obliterate the mind so that I wouldn't be conscious," John explained later. "I think I was maybe suicidal on some kind of subconscious level."

The drinking and the drugs took a terrible physical toll on Harry who, unbeknown to John, was frequently coughing up blood after their wild nights on the town. When they finally made it into the studio, Harry suddenly realized that he had burned his voice out—he could no longer sing.

The shock had sobered both of them, and John suddenly began to take his role as producer seriously. He forced Harry to cut down on his drinking, held him to the house when Ringo, Keith Moon, and the rest went out on their crazy sprees.

Once he had reduced his drinking, John began to think about writing songs again, and he quickly scribbled out a number which, he felt, fitted his circumstances. It was called "Nobody Loves You (When You're Down and Out)." He had a few other ideas in a similar vein, among them a song called "Whatever Gets You Through the Night."

When he had finished *Pussycats,* and Phil Spector had grudgingly posted the rock 'n' roll tapes to him, John became eager to get all his new songs out of his system. He quickly dashed off to New York, asked all his favorite musicians to join him in the recording studio, and banged off a new album called *Walls and Bridges*.

"I'm almost amazed after the year I've been through that I could get anything at all out," he said.

A few weeks later, he played the Spector tapes for the first time and, as he listened, his eyes popped out in horror.

"I didn't even want to hear them, the feelings were so bad about it," he said. "But I listened to them and only about four were savable. The rest were all miles out of tune, just mad; you couldn't use them. Twenty-eight guys all playing out of tune."

He hastily recorded ten more rock 'n' roll songs and then just shelved the whole project.

"There's a jinx on that album," he said. His words were to prove prophetic. Later, when John gave an entrepreneur named Morris Levy a rough tape of the album to listen to, Levy promptly released it under the title *Roots*. John was doubly infuriated because Levy had dug up an old photograph of him with hair over his shoulders for the cover. To counteract the LP, John released his more polished and finished rock 'n' roll album through Capitol. Levy, showing no shame, immediately sued John for $42 million for breach of oral agreement. John was forced to countersue and was eventually awarded $35,000 in damages.

While the case was going on, John had formed a fruitful friendship with Elton John. Elton had simply dropped into the studio while John was hard at work on the *Walls and Bridges* album, and had stayed to jam with John on the "Whatever Gets You Through the Night" track. As a teenager, Elton had worked for Dick James, the Beatles' music publisher, and he had been awed and inspired by John's music. To actually work with John on a song had left Elton feeling ecstatic.

Elton decided at once that he wanted to record one of John's songs and, timorously, he had asked a mutual friend to see if Lennon would consider attending the session. The song Elton chose was "Lucy in the Sky with Diamonds," and John had been delighted not merely to attend, but to sing and play on the record as well.

"Then, again through a mutual friend," said John, "he asked if 'Whatever Gets You Through the Night' got to be number one, would I appear on stage with him, and I said: 'Sure,' not thinking in a million years it was going to get to number one."

Elton John

Predictably, of course, the record hurtled straight to the top of the charts in the autumn of 1974 and, true to his word, John suddenly bounced out onto the stage, dressed all in black, to play with Elton at Madison Square Garden in November. The audience stood on their chairs and screamed for nearly five minutes in near-hysterical welcome for the return of New York's prodigal son.

Few people noticed that John carried a flower in his buttonhole which exactly matched the bloom which Elton wore. Yoko had sent the flowers to the two of them for luck.

As the audience settled back into their seats, John and Elton pounded into "Whatever Gets You Through the Night," "Lucy in the Sky with Diamonds," and finished up with the ancient Beatle hit, "I Saw Her Standing There."

As the final chords died out, the audience and Elton were in tears. Backstage, unbeknown to John, Yoko too was in tears.

"I didn't know she was there," he said later. "I mean, if I had known she was there, I'd just have been too nervous to go on. I would have been terrified. She was backstage afterwards and there was just that moment when we saw each other and like, it's in the movies, you know, when time stands still. And there was silence, everything went silent, and we were just sort of looking at each other and . . . oh, hello . . . and somebody said: 'Well, there's two people in love.' That was before we got back together. But that's probably when we felt something. It was very weird. . . ."

Nevertheless, John's Sinbadlike voyage was not over yet, and he saw the New Year of 1975 in with May Pang in a plush Florida hotel. It was the last time the two of them would ever make love together.

In the spring of 1975, Yoko discovered she was pregnant. The Chinese acupuncturist's prediction had come true.

Bob Mercer, managing director of EMI Records Group Repertoire Division in Britain, was with John discussing details of a possible new record deal when Yoko burst in from her appointment with her doctor, flushed with excitement at the news of her pregnancy.

"Well, Bob," John told him excitedly, "I guess that shelves the work for some time now. I'm going to devote the next nine months to making sure Yoko has this baby. . . ."

Yoko was fragile, and they both wanted this child so badly that John secreted her away in an isolated country house where not even their closest friends could find them. After a few months, her condition became so critical that she moved into a hospital for the remainder of her pregnancy. Even then, though, there were problems—one of which affected John profoundly.

Somebody had given Yoko a transfusion of the wrong blood-type. "I was there when it happened," John would recall later. Yoko quickly grew rigid and began to shake. John found a nurse and told her to get a doctor. While he was holding Yoko, waiting desperately for the doctor to appear, a man came into the room. "He walks in," John related, "hardly notices that Yoko is going through fucking convulsions, goes straight for me, smiles, shakes my hand, and says: 'I've always wanted to meet you, Mr. Lennon. I always enjoyed your music.' I start screaming: 'My wife's dying and you wanna talk about my music!'"

The incident seemed to crystallize John's growing feelings of contempt for his illusory pop star fame.

On October 7, 1975, after three and a half years of legal battles, the United States Court of Appeals canceled the deportation order against John. John's British conviction for possession of marijuana was unjust by U.S. standards, they said. Their decision followed a spate of newspaper revelations about the Nixon administration's Machiavellian plot to deport John because of their fears he would help to disrupt the 1972 Republican Convention. There remained only the formality of awarding John the green card which would allow him to live permanently in the States. (This finally came through on July 27, 1976.)

Two days later, on John's thirty-fifth birthday, Sean Ono Lennon was born into the world, kicking and screaming like a banshee.

One of the Lennons' first visitors when Yoko returned home from the hospital was Bob Mercer. John told him that he wanted to spend the foreseeable future bringing up Sean.

"John wanted to have a close paternal relationship with the child," Mercer related, "and, given the state of his health and wealth, he could afford to do that."

John had read everything he could lay his hands on about parenthood, and he believed that the child's first five years of life were all-important in forming his personality. He would not neglect Sean as he had neglected Julian. He allowed a retrospective anthology of the best of his songs to be released on an album called *Shaved Fish,* and then he and Yoko, quite suddenly, retired from public life. Heinz, the man then responsible for security at the Dakota, was instructed to let no one bother them unless John and Yoko first gave him written instructions. It was a useful ploy, saving John from personally having to tell old friends like Mick Jagger and Elton John that he did not wish to see them. Even Heinz recognized Paul McCartney, however, and he naturally thought John would not wish him to be turned away, and Paul and Linda became frequent visitors.

Awkwardly, John eventually told them he did not wish to see them anymore: "Look," he said, "it's not 1956 and turning up at the door just isn't the same anymore. You know, just give me a ring."

Paul was mortified. Once again, his brittle friendship with John had been dashed.

John seemed to fear he would be drawn away from his family, back into the excitement of making music, if he allowed his old friends back into his home. He was reading heavily now, principally books about anthropology and history—especially the Roman Empire—but also newspapers and current magazines.

16

OLIVIA TRINIDAD ARIAS was born in Mexico and her body seemed to have soaked up some of the sun of that ancient land. Her eyes flashed with fire and her dark hair tumbled around her shoulders like the mane of a lion. But it was her silky voice which had first caught George Harrison's attention in his conversations with her on the telephone. Olivia was then twenty-seven, and she was working in Los Angeles as a secretary for A&M Records—a company George had frequent cause to telephone.

When he met her, he had been astonished. Her gaunt, dark, brooding beauty seemed almost his mirror image: she could have passed for his sister. He called her his dark, sweet lady. Her eyes, he said, shone from the depths of her soul. Somehow, slowly, she pulled him back from the edge of his personal abyss.

George had slipped deeper and deeper into melancholy after Patti's desertion and the failure of his U.S. tour. He poured his misery into two of the gloomiest, most maudlin albums ever released by any rock star: *Dark Horse* and *Extra Texture—Read All About It*. He released a truly dreadful single called "Ding Dong," which became the first single by any Beatle to fail to reach the British top thirty.

It was as though the cloud of libel litigation which hung over his greatest success, "My Sweet Lord," had made him skittish in his writing, and he seemed desperate to make his music sound as far removed from successful pop music as was humanly possible.

"I was so paranoid that I didn't even want to touch my guitar or a piano in case somebody might own the notes I wrote," he admitted later.

The "My Sweet Lord" case finally came to court in January of 1976. The suit was brought by a company called Bright Tunes, Ltd., which claimed that George had simply stolen the tune from the old Chiffons' record "He's So Fine" for his huge hit. The case dragged on for weeks with huge sheets of music draped around the courtroom and an endless stream of experts propounding on whether George had or had not stolen the tune.

George was forced to sit with his guitar in his hands, explaining exactly how he went about composing a song. Essentially, the whole case was a farce.

Almost all rock musicians have borrowed material from other artists, twisting and changing the music, setting new lyrics, so that eventually the source of the final creation was virtually unrecognizable. Nor was there any great shame in this: most successful artists take what has come before as a springboard. To simply conjure up a tune or a painting or a poem from the air, without reference to what has gone before, is likely to create something so radical that the public will not accept it.

In fact, George confessed long after the court case was over, he had ripped off the idea for "My Sweet Lord." But, by cruel irony, he had not been thinking of the melody of "He's So Fine" but of a more recent hit—"Oh, Happy Days," by the Edwin Hawkins Singers. As fate would have it, the tune he so distorted ended up a melody which was virtually identical to "He's So Fine."

Judge Richard Owen accepted that George Harrison had not deliberately plagiarized the song but, he summed up: "It is clear that 'My Sweet Lord' is the very same song as 'He's So Fine.'"

George had copied the melody he said: "because he knew this combination of sounds would work because it already had worked in a song his conscious mind did not remember."

Still the case dragged on until finally, in 1981, George scrawled out a check for $587,000 in damages. His anger was doubly inflamed when he was told that the money would go to the Beatles' former manager, Allen Klein—whose company cannily bought the rights to "He's So Fine" in 1978.

But the "My Sweet Lord" case rapidly paled into insignificance as George became involved in another legal battle in the autumn of 1976—this time with A&M Records.

The fight stemmed from a deal George had signed with A&M in May, 1974, when he was at the peak of his huge post-Beatle popularity. He told the company he was setting up his own Dark Horse label, that he would be signing up some brilliant new artists and that he wanted them to sponsor him.

A&M had been delighted to accept, even though George had told them he would not be able to give them one of his own solo albums until July, 1976, six months after his contract with Apple would be finished.

Although A&M had forked out $2.6 million on Dark Horse, they had been rewarded with just one hit record—Splinter's "Costa Fine Town"—in more than two years. They had watched with increasing concern as George's career had begun to fall apart.

George was confident, however, that his new album, 33⅓, would redress the balance and he blithely flew into Los Angeles a couple of months after his July 26 deadline with the finished master tape.

He had been met with a curt note from Jerry Moss—the "M" in A&M. The new album, George read in horror, was disgracefully overdue. Mr. Moss was very angry—and George was about to be sued for $10 million in damages.

George's already frail health had collapsed completely during his recording of 33⅓. His liver had been damaged by the vast quantities of brandy he had been drinking after the break-up of his marriage and finally, early in 1976, he developed a serious liver infection. The doctor decided to drain poisonous fluid from his body and give him a variety of vitamin supplements. Afterwards, however, he continued to lose weight, and became increasingly weaker.

To Olivia, he seemed to be wasting away in front of her eyes. In desperation, she persuaded him to visit a strange Chinese acupuncturist named Dr. Zion Yu. Dr. Yu, who claims his father was personal physician to Chiang Kai-shek, China's last president before the revolution, numbered many celebrities among his patients, including James Coburn, Jane Fonda, and Robert Blake. Olivia had first met Dr. Yu after her younger brother, Peter, had begun to suffer seizures following a serious motorcycle accident. Doctors said he would simply have to come to terms with life as an epileptic; there was nothing they could do to help him. But Dr. Yu had pushed tiny pins into his body, had massaged his nerve centers, and, within a year, he had been cured.

Dr. Yu had listened patiently to George as he told him of the symptoms he was suffering. He told George there was no problem; he would soon be well again. True to his word, after a few weeks of treatment, George's eyes sparkled, his body pulsed with energy, and, for the first time in more than two years, he began to glow with health.

He realized then that he loved Olivia—as she did him—with a deep, almost spiritual passion. They began going everywhere together, hand-in-hand, giggling like children. She had been genuinely fascinated by Hinduism, eager to become involved with the faith which drove this man she loved with such power.

Their love and his sudden surge of health made it possible for George to effortlessly take the A&M disaster in stride. Calmly, he rang a friend at the rival Warner Brothers record company to explain the situation. After a brief preview of the

33⅓ album, Warners happily agreed to buy off A&M. Then they rush-released the record.

In dramatic contrast to his previous media phobia, George gave scores of radio, television, and newspaper interviews, flashing his freshly capped white teeth at interviewers and dazzling them with his newly rediscovered sense of humor.

"It's a very positive, very up album," he said. "Most of the songs are up; love songs, happy songs. It doesn't compare with the last album, which was a bit depressing."

And, to another interviewer: "I feel sensational—I haven't felt better for two and a half years."

As he jetted from city to city, Olivia held his hand

George at the recording studio

constantly, and provided him with the love and support he so very much needed. At last, like John and Paul, he had found a woman who was his soul mate, the other half to a perfect whole.

In his newfound love, he could not find it in his heart to remember old grievances: "Yes," he said glibly, "of course I'd play with the Beatles if the others wanted to. . . ."

Joyously, he took Olivia to Liverpool, and then to Manchester, where he was to appear on a television talk show with Edward Heath, the former prime minister.

"I see your new book on music is selling well," quipped George, backstage, to the former prime minister. "Do you think you will have to become a tax exile now?"

"Ha, ha, very funny," said Mr. Heath.

The meeting was caught forever by a photographer with an instant film camera. Minutes later, as millions of viewers watched in bewilderment, George appeared on their screens waving the resultant photograph and inviting them to "Spot the loony."

"England needs a bit of cheering up," he grinned later.

When Olivia subtly intimated that she was less than enamored with his vast Los Angeles mansion, with its black-tiled swimming pool, ballroom-sized lounge, and tennis courts, he promptly sold it (for $700,000) to buy a small, quaint, farmhouse-style home in a tranquil corner of Beverly Hills. Life, for George, had never been better.

In January of 1976, Big Mal Evans, the Beatles' former road manager, was in trouble. Mal, who worked so hard and so closely with John, Paul, George, and Ringo that he was almost considered the "fifth Beatle," was stoned out of his brain on pills, waving an air pistol around, screaming of suicide. The woman with him in the room was frightened: the huge, six-foot-three man with the body of a grizzly was out of control. In an adjoining room, the woman's four-year-old daughter was sleeping. When Mal became more and more wild, the woman covertly dialed the police.

Back in the Sixties, Mal had been a strong, gentle, protective giant to the Beatles, pulling over-exuberant fans from Paul's back, smuggling food and dope to them in beleaguered hotel rooms, forging their signatures on photographs for everyone from Prince Charles on down. When the Beatles bought mansions in Surrey, he moved his wife and two children down from Liverpool to buy a place in Sunbury so he could be near them.

In 1967, Mal dropped acid with them, wearing the same long sideburns, beads, floaty scarves. He played harmonica on "Being for the Benefit of Mr. Kite." For "A Day in the Life," Mal had laughingly set an alarm clock to ring after twenty-four bars. The Beatles were so amused that they left it on the record.

When the Beatles went to see the Maharishi, Mal went with them. They wouldn't consider traveling without him. He went with Paul to America to see Jane Asher once, appeared as a magician in the *Magical Mystery Tour* film, wrote articles, and took photographs for the Beatles' fan magazine.

In a cathartic interview in 1970, John described the experience this way: "We took it out on people like Neil, Derek, and Mal. . . . They took a lot of shit from us because we were in such a shitty position. It was hard work and somebody had to take it. These things are left out, you know, about what bastards we were. Fuckin' big bastards, that's what the Beatles were. You have to be a bastard to make it, and that's a fact. And the Beatles are the biggest bastards on earth." Nevertheless, Mal was made a senior executive of Apple. Of all their aides, they loved him best. When it was finally over, however, Mal had all their pain and problems— but not a fraction of their wealth. He was busy for a spell, helping John to overcome his vomiting nervousness backstage in Toronto, dealing with the details for George before the Bangladesh concert at Madison Square Garden. But then there was nothing.

Finally, he had gone to Los Angeles, seeking work as a record producer. His marriage was over and he was lost and lonely and stoned. Maybe the time had come to end it all.

When the L.A. police arrived at the motel, their revolvers drawn, they burst through the door like human juggernauts. Through the haze, Mal heard the door splinter, heard the defeaning roar of their guns, felt the sudden impact of six bullets. And then Big Mal, the "fifth Beatle," was dead.

The four Beatles wept when they heard the news. Not just for Mal, but for themselves. . . .

17

ON MAY 3, 1976, PAUL, about to play his first concert in the U.S.A. in ten years, became so nervous before he went onstage at Fort Worth, Texas, that he could hardly speak. He was only too aware of the savage mauling America had given George, an attack from which Harrison has still not recovered.

"There's no point in getting too hepped up about it," he told a friend. "We'll have to just go out and do the best we can. If it's the end of Wings, then it's the end of Wings."

When the tiny white spotlight finally picked out his face in the blackness of the stage, there was a screaming, sobbing pandemonium—a Beatle had returned from beyond. The show, which had been honed to perfection with years of touring, was brilliant. The audience, holding lighted matches aloft, wept and pleaded for more, while the critics searched their thesauruses for fresh superlatives. For Paul, all the years of pain and anger had at last paid off. The entire tour was greeted with the same acclaim, and the 67,100 people at the Seattle Kingdome broke the record for the largest turnout ever for an indoor concert by a single act. The tour later was turned into both a film and a triumphant triple album. Paul, covered in laurels, returned to Europe to play with concerts at Wembley Arena in London and in Venice's exquisite St. Mark's Square.

Paul arriving at the clinic after James's birth

When, in early 1977, Linda discovered she was pregnant again, Paul scrapped all his concert plans to concentrate on a few projects he had been toying with at home. By far the most successful of these was his ode to his beloved Scotland, "Mull of Kintyre." The record was to become the best-selling single in British history. He also recorded an instrumental album of the music from *Ram* under the pseudonym Percy Thrillington, and helped Denny Laine to put together a solo album of Buddy Holly songs.

For Jimmy McCullough and Joe English, it was a frustrating period. After all the glory of the previous year, Paul seemed to be ignoring them like discarded toys. Occasionally, he would call them out for a brief studio session, but most weeks, there was nothing whatsoever for them to do. Jimmy began drinking vast quantities of alcohol—frequently mixing his drinks with handfuls of pills—in an effort to blot out the boredom.

In September, Linda gave birth to James, her first son. A few weeks later, Jimmy and Joe quit Wings. Jimmy said he planned to join the Small Faces. He was sick of being treated like a session musician; he longed to be part of a real musical team once again.

Paul was unperturbed. He knew that he, Denny, and Linda were the core of Wings. He could always pick up a couple of musicians from somewhere. Besides, Jimmy's drinking had made him a bit of a problem much of the time.

"I am a bit weird," Jimmy had at one time confessed. "Immaturity, I suppose, I've had a lot of experience in music, but experience of life—knowing how to treat people, when to say something and when not to and when you've put your foot in it—I'm still a bit green in that way. . . . Sometimes there's a Jekyll and Hyde within me. Sometimes I really blow it and get on people's nerves."

Paul, in any case, no longer needed to work—other than for his sheer love of making music. His fortune by this time was already approaching $230 million, due partly to the twenty-five percent royalty rate Allen Klein had negotiated for the Beatles. Throughout the Seventies, Beatles' records continued to sell in massive quantities. Even in 1973, long after the break-up, sales of two Beatle compilation albums accounted for an incredible 28.6 percent of EMI's pre-tax music profits. In addition, Paul received a composer's royalty from each of the hundreds of millions of Beatles records that had been sold, plus a performing royalty each time one of their records was played on a jukebox, a radio station, or a TV show. These performing royalties alone would have made him wealthy.

Paul's Wings by this time had sold close to 100 million records around the globe as well, and their concert tour had earned them a small fortune: a single show in Philadelphia during the U.S. tour grossed a fantastic $336,000.

To add to this staggering earning potential, Paul also had the benefit of brilliant investment advice from Lee Eastman. Eastman had persuaded Paul to put a few of his millions into music publishing, with the result that Paul had rapidly become one of the most successful music publishers in the world. His vast catalogue ranged from most of the Buddy Holly songs and Hoagy Carmichael classics to shows like *Hello Dolly; A Chorus Line; Annie;* and *Grease.* Eastman had also advised Paul to line his walls with paintings by Picasso and Magritte.

The paintings gave Paul more pleasure than anything else because he himself was a talented artist. At High Park, he spent much of his time painting views, delighting in the constantly changing light of the Highlands. Yet he remained curiously coy about his work. His painting was one of the few personal activities that was not public knowledge and, for that reason, he held it dear.

One of the few people who has been privileged to see Paul's work is California artist Dane Dickson: "Like a lot of talented people, everything Paul does, he does well," says Dane. "I've no doubt he could make a living out of art if he had to. Paul could even have a one-man show one day—he is that good. But I don't think he's too anxious for anyone to

Paul, with Linda, upon being entered in the Guinness Book of World Records as the world's most successful recording artist, most successful song writer, and the artist who has captured the most gold records

know about his painting. I can't think why. A guy with talent like that shouldn't hide it."

Despite his wealth, the millions of dollars which went astray during the Beatlemania days of the Sixties served to make Paul remarkably thrifty. In recruiting new musicians for Wings, Paul was offering only $450 a week each. Most bands of Wings' caliber worked on profit-sharing schemes which could net musicians as much as $2500 a week.

He eventually found two ambitious young musicians—guitarist Laurence Juber and drummer Steve Holly—who found the salaries adequate.

Linda pantomiming Wings' new Back to the Egg album with Paul

Unfortunately, the slick, professional approach the new Wings attempted to simulate resulted in a truly dreadful album called *Back to the Egg*. The album's only saving grace was a couple of tracks on which Paul teamed together a score of musicians from the Who, Pink Floyd, Led Zeppelin, and Procul Harum to form what he called the Rockestra.

"McCartney has become increasingly involved with the business side of music, and the hours spent in boardrooms can hardly be the ideal environment in which to conceive exciting new material. Instead, it appears to have eroded his musical flair," commented one critic bitchily. The public was not impressed by the record either and it sold badly.

Jimmy McCullough had stayed only briefly with the Small Faces before starting his own new band called the Dukes. Finally, his brother Jack, on September 27, 1979, decided to go to his apartment in London's Maida Vale to see if anything was amiss.

When Jack forced the door of his brother's apartment open, he found the stereo turned on, the apartment neater than he had ever seen it, and Jimmy lying dead on the floor.

Though a pathologist found evidence that Jimmy had been smoking marijuana and drinking alcohol before dying of a huge dose of morphine, there was no trace of alcohol or drugs in the apartment. The mystery deepened when police discovered that a security chain on the front door had been ripped out and that there was no money anywhere.

Police said it seemed almost certain that the apartment had been straightened up after McCullough's death, and yet they could find no one who could help them solve the mystery.

After an open verdict had been recorded at the inquest, Jack McCullough said: "I'm sure someone was in the apartment after my brother died and I'd like to find out who it was."

Paul was upset when he heard the news; despite Jimmy's belligerence, he had remained fond of him.

Paul's life that year was proving unhappy for him in many ways. Linda was growing weary of Wings: she dreaded the thought of going on tour again, of the chaos, the stress, the rigid timetables and the dreadful, phony record company people. They no longer needed the acclaim—couldn't they simply spend more time enjoying themselves as a family, she must have wondered.

Their sheep farm was beginning to produce substantial quantities of wool now. Each year, Paul sheered his huge flock by hand and sent off the fleece to the Wool Marketing Board—though they were somewhat inefficient because of Linda's refusal to allow any of their rams to be slaughtered or castrated. They simply let them wander around together in a special field, like grumpy old gentlemen at a club. Paul and Linda now had a tiny, two-bedroom, Art Nouveau-crammed cottage at Rye in Sussex in addition, where they spent more and more of their time. Yet Paul insisted on spending almost every waking moment hard at work on his multifarious projects.

There was trouble with Heather, too, Linda's daughter by her first marriage. Heather was seventeen now and she resented Paul's domineering attitude toward her. Defiantly, she slashed off her shining, long blonde hair and dyed the remaining stubble in a fashionable punk rainbow. Paul was every bit as appalled as a previous generation of parents had been when their children had grown trim short-back-and-sides Beatle haircuts. He had been even more taken aback when Heather brought home her punk boyfriend who wore a huge armband with the letter "A" on it.

"What does that stand for?" Paul had asked curiously.

"Anarchy."

"What do you mean?"

"The freedom to walk down the street and have no one laugh at the way I dress," Heather's boyfriend replied.

"Oh, no, it isn't," said Paul, sounding for all the world like one of the stern middle-aged parents the Beatles had once derided. "Anarchy means no government, no bus services, no picture shows, and no police."

"Many of the kids just don't know," Paul crowed to another middle-aged friend later.

The Paul McCartney family, 1978

Later, he and Heather had a noisy quarrel in the kitchen of the St. John's Wood house. She had stormed out to tell her friends—most of whom were also children of rich and famous people who had made their homes in London's most expensive suburb.

"You've no need to worry about your dad," they advised her. "If he gives you any more trouble, you can tell the newspapers."

Later, when she and Paul had made up, Heather told him what her friends had said. Paul became visibly shaken.

"Just realizing that she was mixing with children who had this mentality was very worrying," he said.

Within a week, the whole family had abandoned St. John's Wood and moved lock, stock, and barrel to their little cottage at Rye. Heather was enrolled in a local art college and the two younger girls began lessons at the nearby village school. They acquired numerous pets so that, as well as a horse for every member of the family, numerous dogs, and a flock of peacocks, they also had doves, geese, chickens, hamsters, and turtles. Suddenly, they were all close once again. The crisis was over.

They had become very health-conscious—the whole family was vegetarian and Linda grew most of their vegetables in the garden. Paul and Linda still smoked marijuana, but the attitude of the British police toward the drug had mellowed over the years and they rarely went in for raids on people who simply kept a supply for their own use.

Their tranquil peace was interrupted in the autumn of 1979 by a letter from Kurt Waldheim, the secretary-general of the United Nations. Would Paul, he asked, be prepared to play a concert with the rest of the Beatles to raise money for the starving, desperate South Vietnamese refugees? The South Vietnamese were fleeing for their lives in rickety, leaky boats to escape the communist reign of terror precipitated by the withdrawal of the United States.

Paul phoned George and Ringo and they all loosely agreed to appear together as part of a larger group, provided that nothing was leaked to the press in advance. John was not remotely interested. Charity, he felt, began at home. Somehow, though, a newspaper found out what was afoot and the plan was scrapped.

Instead, Paul played a charity concert in London just after Christmas for the people of the ravaged land of Kampuchea. Again, George and Ringo said they might be there—again they shied away when the story was leaked to the press.

Paul also released a single called "Wonderful Christmastime," and toured with Wings in a series of other concerts around England—all hugely successful. But far more importantly, Paul and the rest of Wings were planning one of the biggest tours of their careers: a tour of Japan.

Wings, 1979: Laurence Juber, Paul, Linda, Denny Laine, and Steve Holly

For Paul it was a huge new challenge. Though Japan was second only to the United States as a market for pop records, none of the individual Beatles had played there since their split.

Paul, Linda, and the children paid a brief visit to New York before the tour to exchange Christmas presents with her family. After the break, everyone felt fit and raring to go. The road crew had arranged for the transport of all their equipment and their stage clothes for the eleven sold-out concerts, so that all Linda had to do in the way of packing was to tumble her and Paul's personal bits and pieces into a couple of suitcases.

Stepping out onto the Tarmac at Narita Airport with the children after an exhausting fourteen-hour flight from New York, they were greeted by a fusillade of camera flashes and television arc lights. Paul and Linda waved cheerily to the photographers.

When their luggage arrived, a bespectacled, officious-looking customs man asked them to open their suitcases. Paul smiled sardonically at Linda: it had been years since they had been searched at customs anywhere in the world. She said nothing, but he could see something akin to panic in her eyes.

The first case was opened and there, lying on top of a large pile of clothes, was a plump plastic bag. Paul knew now. The customs man opened the bag, pulling out a little of the innocuous-looking herb to feel and smell it.

Police were called. The children began to cry. They were tired and confused. They couldn't understand what was happening. Handcuffs were snapped around Paul's wrists. Linda looked on speechlessly, beseechingly, as he was led away.

To Paul, confused and suffering jet lag, it all seemed like some ghastly nightmare. Any moment now he would wake up and it would be over. He was driven swiftly through the darkened streets to the police drug control center in central

Tokyo. At midnight the British vice-consul, Mr. Albert Marshall, arrived to see him.

Paul thought he was about to be released.

Mr. Marshall sat down wordlessly, shook his head, and paused. "Well," he said at length, "it could be eight years, you know."

Paul had been charged with attempting to smuggle almost half a pound of marijuana into Japan.

He couldn't sleep at all that night. As he tossed and turned on the hard, thin mattress on the floor of his tiny eight-feet-by-four-feet cell, he couldn't help thinking about being locked away for eight years, about Linda and the kids.

Curiously, a tune kept revolving through his head, a track from an album by Dave Edmunds' Rockpile, and whenever he nearly dozed off, the strident guitar chords seemed to wake him again.

At dawn, a guard came in and ordered him to roll up his mattress and sit cross-legged on a rush mat in the cell for inspection. Paul was frightened. It seemed like a war film.

One by one, a dozen guards wearing identical uniforms and identical faces peered expressionlessly through the wire mesh door.

He was hungry now. About this time, every morning of his life, he had breakfasted on toast, eggs, and cornflakes. But today he was served soya bean soup with rice. It tasted like seaweed and onions.

There had been no wash basin provided; he had washed with water from the lavatory cistern in his cell. It was exactly like a war film. He scratched a thin line on the wall of his cell signifying day one. He remembered that that was what prisoners of war did to keep track of the days.

Moments later, he was handcuffed and hauled off for interrogation.

"Look," he told his inquisitors, "I've already told you it's mine. I'm guilty. What more can I say?"

He was returned to his cell for a lunch of bread, jam, and

Japanese tea, and then handcuffed and hauled off again for a second bout of interrogation. This time, he asked if he could have something to do—his guitar, some books, even a pencil and paper.

His request was later formally refused in a neat letter written on rice paper.

After a dinner of rice and soup, lights were turned out at 8 P.M.

After three days, he began to grow less afraid: the fans were outside calling his name, wishing him well. He tapped on the wall of his cell, began to talk to the other prisoners in pidgin English.

Sometimes he was allowed to take a morning exercise break with the other prisoners. They all knew him, of course, and knew why he had been arrested.

One of them—a man facing a murder charge—holding up seven fingers, told Paul: "You, seven years."

"No, ten," smiled Paul, holding up ten fingers. If nothing else, he had regained his sense of humor.

On the fifth day, Linda had visited him in the bleak, yellow visitors' room.

"I'm so worried," she said. "They say you might get three months."

Paul didn't mention that he could end up with eight years sliced out of his life if the government were to decide to make an example of him.

After a week, he was asked if he wanted a bath. He could either take it alone, they said, or in the prison bathhouse. Paul realized the bathhouse was the nearest thing to a tourist attraction he was going to see on this trip, so he chose to take it there.

The guards gathered in the doorway of the bathhouse as he stripped, curious to see this naked, drug-crazed Beatle.

Paul smiled at them, they grinned back, and suddenly he burst into an impromptu chorus of "Mull of Kintyre." Outside, the fans heard his voice and began to join in, soon followed by other prisoners and the guards. In that moment, Paul illustrated, in a way words never could, the potent magic which had made him one of the world's best-loved entertainers. Naked, imprisoned in a land where no one even spoke his language, he retained that same ability to move people that he had brought to bear on audiences of drunken Germans in Hamburg so many years before. Always, always he had to sing—it was as vital to him as eating, sleeping, or breathing. Small wonder that the possession of this curious magic had driven him to make music so relentlessly for a quarter of a century.

When he was released ten days later, the guards had patted him on the back, and he made a tour of the cells to shake the hands of his fellow prisoners through their food hatches.

The court had ordered, simply, that he should be deported.

"I'll never, ever, smoke cannibis again," he told waiting reporters.

Denny Laine and the other members of Wings had been furious, of course, at the cancellation of the tour. Denny loved being on the road and now, after all the months of preparation, Paul and Linda had stupidly blown the whole thing. For him, it was the final straw—he told Paul he was leaving. He made an angry single without them called "Japanese Tears" and set off on the road with a new band, which included an equally irate Steve Holly.

Paul was devastated: his arrest, the cancellation of the tour, and the break-up of Wings had made this the worst time in his life since the break-up of the Beatles. Now, as then, he withdrew from the world, refused to speak to anyone, and spent his days in exactly the same way he had when the Beatles broke up—recording an album entirely by himself, playing every single instrument, overdubbing, mixing, speaking to no one but Linda about what he was doing.

Denny Laine, however, found he was lost without Paul. He hated the responsibilities and stress of fronting and organiz-

Paul at his Scotland home

ing a band himself, he realized. Shortly afterwards, the two ended their feud—yes, of course Denny could come back to Wings, he'd never really left anyway, had he?

Paul, as part of the promotion for his new solo album, *McCartney II*, had filmed a video of himself wearing different disguises to play each instrument. It seemed obvious that the bass player should be Beatle Paul and so nervously, feeling strange, he had slipped on his old, collarless Beatle jacket, combed his fringe forward, and donned his famous Hofner violin bass guitar. Looking down, he noticed that the list of songs he had played during the *Let It Be* concert on the roof of Apple's building was still taped to it.

"And then, a few days later, it hit me," he said. "I'd finally gone and broken the whole Beatles voodoo. . . ."

Coincidentally, it was almost exactly ten years since Paul had finally revealed to the world that their best-loved band had broken up.

=18=

JOHN AND YOKO symbolically cleansed themselves of their past early in 1976 by fasting for six weeks, during which time they drank only Japanese tea and fruit juices.

Thereafter, they occasionally ate in nearby Japanese restaurants, particularly one called the Lenge, where the simple rice and fish dishes accommodated their macrobiotic diet. The waiters in these restaurants were astonished to discover that John now spoke fluent Japanese—a language Yoko had helped him to learn from books.

While Yoko toiled over their complex tangle of business affairs, John rose at six each morning to drink Japanese tea and to prepare Sean's breakfast. He taught himself to bake bread, a feat which he found quite as demanding as making a record. Eventually, however, like many housewives, he became bored.

Yoko, sensing his boredom, suggested he take a holiday on his own: it would do him good, she would enjoy looking after Sean by herself for a while. At first, he had been terrified: he had never traveled anywhere without Big Mal Evans, Anthony Fawcett, or some similar aide to organize the details, cope with the fans, to generally cushion him.

All the more reason, insisted Yoko, for him to try it now.

Somehow, reluctantly, he booked himself on a jet to Hong Kong and when, upon arriving, he finally slammed the door of his hotel room behind him, he was quaking with nerves. It was the first time for almost twenty years that he had had to actually organize such a trip. He had never before checked into a hotel, never had to even bother to actually call room service himself. There had always been someone there to do it for him. Even unpacking his suitcase was a fresh experience. He needed a Valium or a drink, but instead he took a long, hot bath. Yoko maintained that a bath was the best sedative of all. Timorously, he gazed out of his window at the chaotic, seething streets, steeling himself for the moment when he would venture outside.

Repeatedly, though, his nerve failed him. Each time, he would simply take another bath and escape into a book or the television.

Eventually, early one morning, he simply strolled out of the hotel, looking neither to the left nor the right. He followed a bustling crowd of bleary-eyed office workers onto a packed ferry boat. Nobody noticed him, nor even looked at him: there are very few millionaire superstars on the early-morning boats across Hong Kong Bay. When he arrived in Kao Lung, he simply dropped into a tea house and ordered breakfast: an everyday tourist morning. But, for John, it was a momentous experience. He felt like a teen-ager on his first trip abroad spreading his wings and fluttering from the nest. In that moment, he realized he had rediscovered himself: he had endured all the Beatlemania, the Indian mysticism, the drugs, and the women to return to the same point in his life he had been at when he started out in Liverpool over twenty years before.

Thereafter he, Yoko, and Sean traveled widely to Japan, to South Africa, and even to Spain. Once, in Spain, the three of them sat sipping cold drinks in a small, sunny café and, from the way the waiters were nudging one another and staring in his direction, John realized that he had at last been recognized. Suddenly, a gypsy violinist strolled across and began to serenade them with "Yesterday"—Paul's most famous Beatle song. John laughed uproariously, until the tears streamed down his face.

"Well, they could hardly have played 'I Am the Walrus,' could they?" he joked later.

With the final settling of the Beatles' affairs—due largely to Yoko's doggedness and imagination—John was earning more than $12 million each year in assorted royalties. Yoko was advised that, since inflation was throwing the money-markets into turmoil, they should invest in land and property. She and John bought themselves a little farm in the foothills of the Catskill Mountains.

Valley View Farm was a three hundred and sixteen acre spread near the village of Franklin. The white farmhouse stood at the end of a narrow snow-lined road, heavily posted with signs warning off trespassers and hunters. The sixty-year-old building looked distinctly shabby outside, with green paint peeling from the porch ceiling and dangling gray wires instead of an overhead light near the front steps of the faded, gray barn. When they were at the farm, John, Yoko, and Sean deliberately cut themselves off from neighboring farmers and actively discouraged visitors.

By June of 1979, the world was clamoring to know what John was doing: he had become mysterious in his reclusiveness.

In response, John and Yoko published the following letter in several newspapers under the heading: "A LOVE LETTER FROM JOHN AND YOKO TO PEOPLE WHO ASK US WHAT, WHEN, AND WHY":

> The past ten years, we noticed everything we wished came true in its own time, good or bad, one way or the other. We kept telling each other that one of these days we would have to get organized and wish for only good things. Then our baby arrived! We were overjoyed and at the same time felt very responsible. Now our wishes would also affect *him*. We felt it

was time for us to stop discussing and do something about
our wishing process: The Spring Cleaning of our minds! It
was a lot of work. We kept finding things in those old closets
in our minds that we hadn't realized were still there, things
we wished we hadn't found. As we did our cleaning, we also
started to notice many wrong things in our house: there was a
shelf which should never have been there in the first place, a
painting we grew to dislike, and there were two dingy rooms,
which became light and breezy when we broke the walls
between them. We started to love the plants, which one of us
originally thought were robbing the air from us! We began to
enjoy the drumbeat of the city, which used to annoy us. We
made a lot of mistakes and still do. In the past, we spent a lot
of energy in trying to get something we thought we wanted,
wondered why we didn't get it, only to find out that one or
both of us didn't really want it. One day, we received a sudden
rain of chocolates from people around the world. "Hey, what's
this! We're not eating sugar stuff are we?" "Who's wishing
it?" We both laughed. We discovered that when two of us
wished in unison, it happened faster. As the Good Book
says—Where two are gathered together—it's true. Two is
plenty. A Newclear Seed.

More and more we are starting to wish and pray. The
things we have tried to achieve in the past by flashing a "V"
sign, we try now through wishing. We are not doing this
because it is simpler. Wishing is more effective than waving
flags. It works. It's like magic. Magic is simple. Magic is real.
The secret of it is to know that it is simple, and not kill it with
an elaborate ritual, which is a sign of insecurity. When
somebody is angry with us, we draw a halo around his or her
head in our minds. Does the person stop being angry then?
Well, we don't know! We know, though, that when we draw a
halo round a person, suddenly the person starts to look like an
angel to us. This helps us to feel warm toward the person,
reminds us that everyone has goodness inside, and that all
people who come to us are angels in disguise, carrying

messages and gifts to us from the Universe. Magic is logical. Try it sometime.

We still have a long way to go. It seems the more we get into cleaning, the faster the wishing and receiving process gets. The house is getting very comfortable now. Sean is beautiful. The plants are growing. The cats are purring. The town is shining, sun, rain, or snow. We live in a beautiful universe. We are thankful every day for the plentifulness of our life. This is not a euphemism. We understand that we, the city, the country, the earth are facing very hard times, and there is panic in the air. Still the sun is shining and we are here together, and there is love between us, our city, our country, the earth. If two people like us can do what we are doing with our lives, any miracle is possible! It's true we can do with a few big miracles right now. The thing is to recognize them when they come to you and to be thankful. First they come in a small way, in everyday life, then they come in rivers, and in oceans. It's goin' to be all right. The future of the earth is up to all of us.

Many people are sending us vibes every day in letters, telegrams, taps on the gate, or just flowers and nice thoughts. We thank them all and appreciate them for respecting our quiet space, which we need. Thank you for all the love you send us. We feel it every day. We love you, too. We know you are concerned about us. That is nice. That's why you want to know what we are doing. That's why everybody is asking us What, When and Why. We understand. Well, this is what we've been doing. We hope that you have the same quiet space in your mind to make your own wishes come true.

If you think of us next time, remember, our silence is a silence of love and not of indifference. Remember, we are writing in the sky instead of on paper—that's our song. Lift your eyes and look up in the sky. There's our message. Lift your eyes again and look around you, and you will see that you are walking in the sky, which extends to the ground. We are all part of the sky, more so than of the ground. Remember, we love you.

> John Lennon and Yoko Ono
> May 27, 1979
> New York City

P.S. We noticed that three angels were looking over our shoulders when we wrote this!

For many, the letter merely confirmed the rumors about John's reclusive eccentricity.

John and Yoko had been so enamored with their Valley View Farm that they began to pump much of their surplus cash into it and, before long, they bought three more dairy farms around Franklin and the nearby township of Delhi. Their arrival was not welcomed with open arms by their new neighbors, however. Dairyman Philip Ackerman spoke for many when he protested: "It's a tax shelter, pure and simple. What concerns us as farmers is that if New York City's money owns all these big farms at a tax loss, what's going to happen if they change the laws so that people like the Lennons lose their tax advantage?

"You see, absentee owners then sell the property at low prices and that will drive seed and farm machinery dealers out of business and deflate property values in the country. People like the Lennons make it virtually impossible for young people to break into farming in the county unless they already have a family farm to take over."

Undeterred, John and Yoko continued to invest their money in farms and in palatial mansions at Palm Beach and on Long Island. By 1980, their dairy herd had become one of the finest in the U.S. Its value was estimated at $60 million and they once sold a single cow for $250,000. In addition, they purchased every apartment which became vacant in the

Dakota—seven in all—and amassed a multimillion-dollar collection of ancient Egyptian artwork. When the *New York Post* suggested that their total fortune was worth in excess of $150 million, neither John nor Yoko argued.

Yet, astonishingly, John saw no contradiction between his incredible wealth and his songs of fraternity and equality.

"In England, there are only two things to be, basically: You are either for the labor movement or for the capitalist movement," he explained. "Either you become a right-wing Archie Bunker if you are in the class I am in, or you become an instinctive socialist, which I was. That meant I think people should get their false teeth and their health looked after, all the rest of it. But apart from that, I worked for money and I wanted to be rich. So what the hell—if that's a paradox, then I'm a socialist. But I am not anything. What I used to be is guilty about money. That's why I lost it, either by giving it away or by allowing myself to be screwed by so-called managers."

That summer, as Sean approached his fifth birthday and John his fortieth, John bought a small sailing ship called *Strawberry Fields,* and the two of them sailed to Bermuda together with Sean's nanny, a housekeeper, and a full crew of sailors. Yoko remained behind in New York.

Before he left, John had begun recording his comeback album. This time, he and Yoko would sing on alternate tracks: they wanted to tell the world how much they loved and needed one another, how happy they had become with Sean.

One day, as John, Sean, and their entourage sat down to lunch in Bermuda's Botanical Gardens, John noticed a singularly beautiful flower. It was called Double Fantasy.

"That's it," John realized. "The perfect title for the album."

When he returned, he and Yoko polished the album together in the Hit Factory Studio in New York.

It was released to glowing reviews and huge advance sales that autumn. John babbled excitedly: he would return to

Liverpool again, he would show Aunt Mimi her grandson for the first time, he would play concerts.

He was, most friends agreed, happier than he had been since the first days of the Beatles. . . .

19

GEORGE'S NEW ZEST FOR LIFE, sparked by his love for Olivia, revived an early passion for fast cars. One day, he exchanged his utilitarian BMW for a gleaming, 150 M.P.H. Porsche. In May of 1977, after 33⅓ had sold more than a million copies, he and Olivia drove the new car onto a cross-channel ferry and meandered slowly through France to meet up with Ringo and his girlfriend, Nancy Andrews, to watch the Monte Carlo Grand Prix.

Before long, he had purchased a couple more Porsches and a Ferrari from Rodney Turner, who ran a car showroom close to George's home in Henley-on-Thames.

"Hardly a month seems to go by without us having to make the garage bigger," grumbled George's brother good-naturedly.

Not surprisingly, George's collection of cars led to a temptation to occasionally flout Britain's 70 M.P.H. speed limit. When the urge proved overwhelming, George, Rodney, and one or two other friends would race one another at speeds of up to 145 M.P.H. on a ten-mile circuit of remote country lanes not far from Henley. After one race, a friend frightened George by sending him a spoof telegram stating he had been spotted by the police driving at something approaching the speed of sound. George roared with relief when they told him what they had done. He had the telegram framed.

He also delighted in dropping in to simply talk cars with Rodney at his showroom.

"I can remember once George and I were sitting in the showroom reading magazines and laughing about something," related Turner, "when a Harley Street eye specialist, who is a friend of mine, dropped by to look at my eyes—after I had had some trouble with them. George looked slightly askance at this man gazing into my eyes, but he just carried on chatting about his Ferrari and asking me if I had any bits for it.

"'Look, George,' I told him, 'if you're really anxious to get them now, go and have a look in the rubbish bin out the back, you might find something that will fit there.'

"At this, the old doctor looked round, obviously thinking that George was a singularly scruffy-looking individual, and he asked him: 'Are you in the scrap metal business by any chance?'

"George roared with laughter and I explained: 'Oh, I'm terribly sorry, you haven't met George Harrison—he played in a group called the Beatles. . . .'"

Interwoven with George's passion for driving and talking about cars was an ever-increasing interest in car-racing. He became friendly not just with racing stars like Jackie Stewart, Ronnie Peterson, Barry Sheene, and James Hunt, but also with the mechanics and engineers who toiled away behind the scenes. So dogged was his fan worship that some crews, joking affectionately about him, dubbed him the "pits groupie." Any malice, though, invariably evaporated when they met him and saw the sincerity of his enthusiasm.

Former world champion driver Jackie Stewart was among those who were especially impressed. Stewart's own success on the track coincided with the height of Beatlemania and he still remembered the Beatle record at the top of the charts that coincided with each of his victories. The Beatles provided the soundtrack for his life, just as they did for everyone else who was young during the Sixties.

George Harrison and Jackie Stewart

"I guess I must have been the world's greatest Beatle fan," Stewart said. "I mean, I would have given my right arm to have met any of them. Then when I met George at the Long Beach Grand Prix in California, I was impressed at how mellow and modest he was. And I was amazed to discover that he was more knowledgeable about my racing career than I was—though maybe I was more knowledgeable about his career than he was. Anyway, it was nice because nobody had to try to impress anyone else."

Though George had no wish to become involved in the business side of motor-racing, he did agree to generously pay more than $25,000 to help sponsor twenty-five-year-old Grand Prix motorcyclist Steve Parrish.

Once George drove the vintage Lotus 18, in which Stirling Moss had won a Monte Carlo Grand Prix many years before, in a charity race at Britain's Donington Racetrack. Pitted against George in other classic, old racing cars were such celebrities as Jackie Stewart, James Hunt, and Mario Andretti.

"I was sitting there, trying not to let the engine stall, and suddenly they all shot away," said George afterwards.

He shuddered and lurched his way around the track and when marshalls waved yellow warning flags at him, he simply waved back.

"Well, I haven't got much chance against that bunch, have I?" he explained.

Jackie Stewart thought George's passion for motor-racing stemmed from his longing for the extremes of excitement he experienced with the Beatles and, immediately afterwards, with his concert for Bangladesh.

"He is still enjoying his success, but in a highly moderated way," as Jackie described it.

Sadly, the essence of motor-racing's excitement stems from its proximity to disaster, as evidenced when Niki Lauda was trapped in his blazing Ferrari after a horrific crash at Nürburgring in 1976. Niki suffered hideous burns to his face

George, indulging his passion for race-car driving

and body, and had breathed in clouds of toxic fumes; soon after his arrival at a nearby hospital, a priest, fearing the worst, gave him the last rites.

Six weeks later, swathed in bandages so that he looked like a prized creation of Doctor Frankenstein, Lauda returned to the racetrack and ended the season just one point behind James Hunt, the new world champion.

George was awed by this chilling ability to overcome all adversity. Lauda became an even closer friend thereafter.

Not all crashes end in glorious comebacks, however. George walked around in a daze for nearly a month after the death of his friend, Ronnie Peterson, during the Italian Grand Prix at Milan in 1978. A few months later, when

George heard that his friend, motorcycle champion Barry Sheene, was seeking a backer who would put up about $350,000 to enable him to start racing Grand Prix cars, George offered to pay Sheene £150,000 *not* to begin Formula One racing.

During this time, George became a popular regular at a local pub, the Row Barge. On his first visit to the pub, a few of the regulars had stared at him curiously. But when one of them challenged him to a game of darts, he suddenly was accepted. Thereafter, he frequently strolled into the pub for a pint, a game of darts, and a chat, just as his father and his grandfather had always done in Liverpool. Norman and Dot Mitchell, who ran the pub, became close friends.

One evening, George invited them both to join him at Friar Park for a dinner party. He served copious goblets of vintage Champagne and spicy, vegetarian Hindu food cooked by a nephew of Ravi Shankar, named Khuma, who had now become George and Olivia's personal assistant at Friar Park.

Afterwards, all the guests went down to the underground river to merrily row boats through the caves. Inevitably, there was much skylarking and splashing: "Well," says Norman, "I think George was in a bit of a comical mood and he started rocking the boat from side to side. I tried to lean over to help somebody in the next boat and I leaned over too far and there was an almighty splash. I struck out in my best Mark Spitz style, made about four strokes, and I was back on the bank."

Thereafter, George and Olivia became firm friends of Norman and Dot. They went out to restaurants together—where Norman was impressed at George's patience with the autograph hunters who persistently interrupted his meal. On Dot's birthday, George strolled into the Row Barge alone. He called her to one side and, teasingly, told her to hold out her hand and close her eyes; he dropped three perfect, invaluable rubies into her hands. "Have a nice birthday," he told her.

George's generosity was well known. On June 7, 1977, the day of the Queen's Silver Jubilee, George attended a street party in Henley where he presented every child with a souvenir goblet, then left enough money behind the bar to buy a drink for every adult.

George also occasionally took it into his head to buy a drink for every person who happened to be in the Row Barge. But instead of flaunting his money ostentatiously, he would call Norman into a corner of the bar, give him the money, and ask him to tell the customers that it was somebody's birthday.

Offers by promoters to pay George enormous sums of money, however, were politely declined. On one occasion, the newspapers were full of a fatuous £5 million offer (about $12 million) for the Beatles to re-form for a single concert. In the midst of all the fuss, George slipped into the Row Barge with a bag of fish and chips he had just purchased from a nearby shop.

"Here, Norm," said George, who was being offered $3 million for an hour's work, "do you mind if I eat these in here? They'll get cold if I have to walk all the way up to my driveway with them."

That evening, Norman, in a farcical mood, popped off a check to George for £5 million and 50p with a request that the Beatles play their comeback show in the Row Barge.

"Well, that's okay," George told him. "I've got mine. But John, Paul, and Ringo want to know how much they're going to get."

"Oh, no," laughed Norman. "I can't afford £5 million and 50p each—that's just too much."

Another of George's friends at this time was a teen-aged local newspaper reporter named David Coxwell—whom he used to tease by calling him "Scoop."

"I went up there to talk to him for an article I was writing about Sir Frank Crisp," says David. "But somehow we got talking about music and Bob Dylan and suddenly he started teaching me all sorts of little tricks to play certain chords. It was the most amazing lesson I have ever had. And, afterwards, I simply dashed home to practice what he had taught me. I completely forgot about Sir Frank with all the excitement."

George's next project involved yet another, far closer, friend. When George heard that Eric Idle, star of Monty Python's Flying Circus, was finding it impossible to obtain backing for the Monty Python film *The Life of Brian,* he promptly offered to put up half the money needed—$5½ million. It turned out to be the finest investment of his life, because when *The Life of Brian* became a box-office smash around the world, George reaped a profit of more than $65 million.

George's passion for Pythonesque humor showed yet another facet of his extraordinary and contradictory personality.

"Well, I am two-faced," he is fond of joking.

"But really," he adds, "things serious and comical are like night and day, black and white, *yin* and *yang.* In order to be comical, you have to be serious. You can't have one without the other. The world is a very serious and, at times, very sad place—but at other times it is all such a joke. . . ."

Idle, confirming George's humorous side, called him one of the funniest people he knew. "He likes a good laugh and a good giggle quite as much as anyone." But, most of all, Idle thought that George wanted to lead a complete, full life. "He's one of the few morally good people that rock 'n' roll has produced. He has turned his attentions into goodness and being good and he's extremely generous and he backs and supports all sorts of people that you'll never know, ever hear of. Because he just gives away money and supports them. He's just a wonderful bloke.

"George has never been the sort of bloke who goes around in saffron robes, you know, he's interested in goodness and spiritual values and whatever is of worth and merit in the world and he does a lot of good things that are missed by the White House form of Christianity that passes for Christianity in this part of the world."

This very openness and generosity, however, have occasionally made George the target of many cranks. For several months, members of the insidious Moonies sect lay siege to

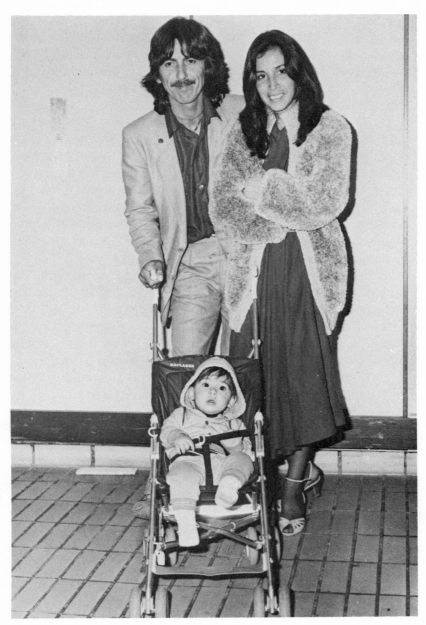

George, Olivia, and their son, Dhani

Friar Park, slipping into the gardens when no one was about and pestering George each time he ventured out. Eventually, Harry Harrison, who has the physique of a professional wrestler, firmly persuaded them to find a new target for their affections.

On August 1, 1978, Olivia Arias gave birth to George's son. The two decided to name him Dhani—the Indian word for wealthy—and George was suddenly thrown into paroxysms of joy. He rushed to Rodney Turner to order a Rolls-Royce— "blue for boy"—so their son would not be unduly jostled on his journey home from the hospital. Four weeks later, without a word to anyone—not even George's brothers— George and Olivia were married secretly by special license at Henley Register Office.

At first, George was so protective of his new son that he refused to take him outside the grounds of Friar Park. He would not allow anyone to even touch the child.

"I was a bit surprised," his brother said. "I mean, I've got two kids of my own. But it must have been three or four months before he would even let me touch the baby."

To George, the child was more precious than rubies. After all the fame, the adulation, the money, and the mysticism, he at last found himself in the simplicity of his family's love. He would still, he decided, make an album every couple of years. But, like John, all he really wanted from life now was to watch his son grow. . . .

20

LIKE GEORGE AND JOHN, Ringo too suffered through the throes of divorce. In this, the Beatles, as always, seemed to mirror the times, just as they had mirrored the joyous, youthful bubbling of the early Sixties and the philosophical questioning at the end of that decade. Society in the Seventies experienced an unprecedented breakdown of marriage in the Western world. In Britain, there were nearly six times as many divorces in 1979 as there were in 1960. It seemed as if many people, taught to seek personal fulfillment, to live always for themselves, now believed that they could chase down their elusive happiness simply by changing partners.

For John and George, divorce had, indeed, been a prelude to lives of new concordance. But for Ringo, it had been like the severing of a string which holds a kite to earth, and, thereafter, he had seemed to simply flutter around with the breeze, wherever the wind blew him.

His first move on being divorced had been to pay Maureen a generous settlement of over $1,000,000. His second was to flee the punitive taxes of England to set up home among the rich, elderly tax exiles of Monte Carlo. He bought an apartment in a ghastly modern block glowering over the rocky principality and set up home there with Nancy Andrews, an American model.

Ringo and Nancy Andrews in 1975

Though he occasionally played his piano and his guitar and watched video films sent over from England, the days became soporifically boring. In the evenings, he and Nancy would eat at frighteningly expensive restaurants, usually with middle-aged, exiled Britons. Then, about four evenings each week, they would gamble, usually at the fashionable Loews Casino. Ringo played blackjack, and occasionally roulette—but always for modest stakes.

"He's well-known around Monte Carlo and people treat him very much as a star, which is something he seems to enjoy," said Loews' manager Paul Maser of Ringo. "He's still a little outrageous sometimes—like a little while back he turned up here with his hair in a ponytail. But, overall now, he seems to be a typical retired English gentleman.

"He is exactly like someone who has spent years working extremely hard to build up a business, becoming a multi-millionaire, and who is now sitting back, enjoying the fruits of success. When he walks around Monte Carlo now, people notice him and point him out, but they don't go running for autographs like they used to. Let's face it, he's hardly a sexy, young, pop star anymore, is he?"

Before long, Nancy grew weary of Monte Carlo's indolence and returned home to the States, leaving Ringo to toy with the idea of finding some form of occupation. He decided to set up his own record label, which he called Ring'O Records, and to sign Bobby Keyes and a few other friends who he thought deserved a chance to show what they could do on record.

"Then I realized to run the company, you've got to be in the company," he said later. "You've got to come to the office every day, which I did. And you've got to go and have all those meetings, which I hated, because you'd have all these meetings and nothing would happen. You usually have meetings to decide about the next meeting. So I did tend to leave it alone—and then I just decided I didn't want it no more: 'I'm getting out of here. . . .'"

The company was revived a little while later, after Ringo signed a new deal to release his own records thorugh Polydor in Britain and Atlantic in the States. This time, Ringo, however, asked a friend to run Ring'O Records for him—with disastrous results.

"I think we had some good artists," he reflected. "But maybe we were the only ones who thought they were any good. Well, the people outside didn't think they were that terrific because they didn't buy their records and that is what a record company is all about. If you don't sell records, then it costs you money. So when it costs you a certain amount of money, you have to look at it straight and say: 'What's going on?' And you either turn it around or you do as I did and decide, yet again, that it is time for it to end."

Meanwhile, Ringo's own recording career was also slip-sliding away from him. His first album under the new deal with Polydor was called *Ringo's Rotogravure,* and Ringo undertook an exhausting campaign of newspaper, radio, and television interviews to help to turn it into a modest success. The experience was so abhorrent to him that he virtually refused to promote his two follow-up LPs.

"Ringo just seemed content to let the producer lay down some backing tracks for him and then he would pop in from Monte Carlo or wherever and just stick on his vocals," said Tony Bramwell, who worked for Apple before becoming a senior executive with Polydor. "We had many offers for TV series, specials, and whatever for him, but he was always totally unavailable to do them. He didn't seem to have much commitment to make and sell good albums."

Not surprisingly, the records sold in ever-diminishing quantities and Polydor eventually decided not to renew Ringo's contract.

"The record company is not going to control my artistic life," argues Ringo. "I can give them the records and they can sell them if they can. They kept asking me to do these shows all over the world, but at that point I didn't want to do it. I just didn't want to get into that situation."

Ringo also set up a record production company called the Able Label—but that, too, soon faded into obscurity. A major factor in his lack of interest in work and business seemed to be a feeling that the sands of time were running out for him. So many of his close friends were dying: Marc Bolan, Keith Moon, Mal Evans—always in such tragic circumstances.

Ringo's own health had been poor since, at the age of six, he developed appendicitis. His appendix burst, and he was in a coma for ten weeks, in the hospital for twelve months. Then, when he was thirteen, he developed chronic pleurisy. This time, he was hospitalized for two years. Throughout his years with the Beatles, he had become ill several times and had to be hospitalized for further operations.

In grim fulfillment of Ringo's forebodings, in April of 1979, he collapsed in a coma in Monte Carlo. To save his life, doctors were forced to remove five feet of his intestines. He was, they said afterwards, very lucky to be alive.

"I won't go to funerals because I don't believe in them," he said later. "I totally believe your soul has gone by the time you get into the limo. She or he's up there or wherever it is. I'm sure . . . I can't wait to go half the time."

After his recovery, he gently slipped into the life of an international playboy. He bought houses in Amsterdam and Los Angeles. He romanced such beautiful women as actresses Viviane Ventura and Shelley Duvall, and "Top of the Pops" star Samantha Just. After a long dalliance with singer Lynsey de Paul, he bought her a fishing rod, because, he said, she was always fishing for compliments.

"Well, I am a jet-setter," he admitted lugubriously. "Whatever anyone may think and whoever puts it down, I am on planes half the year going to different places. And, in people's eyes, Monte Carlo is a jet-set scene. Los Angeles is a jet-set scene. London—swinging London, not that it swings anymore. Amsterdam, you know. It's a crazy kind of a world. Wherever I go, it's a swinging place, man.

"I like the position I'm in where I can do what I want to do. But, of course, occasionally, they force me to work and then, occasionally, I force everyone else to work. When I want to do something, I have my little tantrums when I say: 'Why don't we all do this?' And they all go: 'Oh, god, he's off again. . . .'"

Ringo's "little tantrums" frequently came as a surprise to those who still thought of him as the cute, funny, cuddly Beatle.

"He doesn't want to be thought of as a clown anymore," revealed Ringo's mother, Mrs. Elsie Graves. "He's more serious than most people realize and he can be forceful when he needs to be. I don't think he has yet really achieved the things he wants to achieve. More than anything, he wants to become successful on his own terms as an actor. I don't think he has really fulfilled himself yet."

Despite Ringo's jet-setting life, he retained a passionate love for his three children. He signed Tittenhurst Park—

Ringo and singer Lynsey de Paul

which had been valued roughly at $1.7 million—over to them, together with the income the property earned from its busy recording studio. And when Maureen told him she thought the family would be happier living closer to the center of town, he bought them a $600,000 house in North London.

In May of 1980, Ringo's jet-setting life-style almost came to a jet-setting halt as he rolled his Mercedes over and over on a highway at Kingston, Surrey, with the woman he was dating, Barbara Bach, the beautiful blonde co-star of the James Bond film *The Spy Who Loved Me*, by his side. As the somersaulting car demolished three lampposts, Ringo was thrown clear but Barbara was trapped inside. Miraculously, the two of them suffered only slight cuts and bruises. Ringo decided that if they could survive this they could survive anything together, and he promptly asked Barbara—who had two children of her own—to marry him. Ringo had the Mercedes crushed into a cube, which they planned to use as a coffee table in their new home. Romantic Ringo had two chunks of the broken windshield set in gold and fashioned into brooches to remind him of the day they cheated death.

"I'm incredibly happy now," Barbara remarked breathlessly later as she posed naked for *Playboy*. "I had always secretly believed in Prince Charming, if ever he came riding up on his charger. And Richard came. We'll get married, and that's it . . . happily ever after, all the rest. So now I'm into fairy tales."

Nancy Andrews, less than impressed, promptly sued Ringo for more than $7 million in a palimony suit.

Ringo had first met his Barbara when they filmed the comedy spoof, *Caveman*, together.

"I used to get offered film parts just because I was an ex-Beatle," Ringo said. "But that doesn't happen any more and now, with *Caveman*, I'll either make it on my own terms or I will end up with egg all over my face."

Beatlemania, meanwhile, continued unabated throughout the Seventies. When EMI rereleased a selection of Beatles'

Ringo and Barbara Bach

Ringo in Caveman, *1981*

singles in 1976 they totally dominated the charts, finally achieving twenty-three records in the British top one hundred. Every one of their compilation albums was a huge success. A Beatlemania stage show was successful throughout the world and there were numerous other stage, film, and record spin-offs.

"Well, who else is there?" said Ringo of the Beatles' continuing popularity. "There's nobody else. You couldn't have 'Elton John Week'—even though Reg is a very nice lad, when he wants to be. They do Elvis and they do us. Everyone

can relate to the Beatles, you know, children who weren't
born relate through the music.

"We always did songs which related to everybody from
children to our parents and grandparents. And now we're the
the parents and my mother is a grandparent and she still
relates. I mean, the melody lingers on—everyone relates to
'Yesterday' and half the people still relate to 'I Am the
Walrus.' We were the monsters. There's been a lot of biggies,
and very few monsters. That's the difference."

Over the years, as the world looked back with increasing
nostalgia on the salad days of the Sixties, there were ever
larger offers for a Beatle reunion. But when even Ringo, the
poorest Beatle, had more millions lying around than he knew
what to do with, money was no longer very tempting or
relevant to their life-styles. Only love could bring them
together. . . .

On May 19, 1979, Eric Clapton celebrated his marriage to
George Harrison's former wife, Patti, with a huge party for all
his friends on the grounds of Hurtwood Edge. The wedding
took place two months previously at a small church in
Tucson, but this was the first opportunity they had to stage
their belated reception. Mick Jagger attended, as did David
Bowie. During the evening, a few guests nudged one another
to point at the three men sipping drinks together around a
table, growing starry-eyed in retelling tales of their illustrious
past. George, Paul, and Ringo have lived a lifetime mere
mortals can only dream of. The antipathy and the rivalry
were long gone now: George was essentially a gardener,
Ringo a playboy—only Paul still played at being a pop star.
Ten years after the break-up, they could forget the backbiting and remember the good times: the girls in Hamburg; the
night John tried to mug a drunken sailor. They roared with
laughter together like old warriors.

Their children grew bored with the tales of yesterday and
wandered away to play with instruments which had been left

Eric Clapton and the former Patti Harrison, following their marriage on March 27, 1979

lying on a makeshift stage at one end of the grounds. Ringo's son, Zak, was developing into a superb drummer.

Then, suddenly, almost magically, Paul, George, and Ringo were on stage together—soon joined by Denny Laine, Eric Clapton, and a host of others.

"Hey," giggled one of the guests, "it's a Beatles reunion."

Together they ploughed through "Sgt. Pepper's Lonely Hearts Club Band" and other old Beatle hits, ancient Chuck Berry and Little Richard rock 'n' roll classics. Paul, George, and Ringo held the stage, dominated the show. The rest of the musicians were content simply to play backing rhythms and sing harmonies.

"And, no, it didn't feel strange at all," claimed Paul. "We were having a booze-up and a laugh and suddenly we were playing together again. It felt pretty good to me. . . ."

Later, as their chauffeurs helped them into their limousines, they were all laughing and joking, high with the fun of being together, of feeling young once again.

"Oh, yeah," Paul agreed, "it'll be great to do one like that again with just the four of us, once Sean is five and John starts playing again. . . ."

"I USED TO
WORRY . . ."

21

THE YOUNG MAN with the pudgy face and the strange, vacant stare tugged the woolen scarf tied tightly around his neck and unbuttoned his thick overcoat. There were small beads of perspiration on his forehead and his plastic-framed, tinted spectacles slipped uncomfortably down his nose. With an unseasonably warm wind blowing through New York, it felt more like spring than December, making a mockery of the secretaries and clerical workers who bustled along the busy streets grasping the precious, gift-wrapped paraphernalia of Christmas in their arms. The man looked about twenty-five. He was not ugly, merely nondescript. He merited no second glance from the skittering passersby as he loitered idly outside the hideously ugly Gothic apartment building on Central Park West and 72nd Street.

Beneath his arm, the man clutched an LP record. He held it as though it was something sacrosanct, almost as though he feared someone might attempt to snatch it away from him. The front cover was filled with a black-and-white photograph of a man and a woman gently kissing. They seemed somehow sublime, almost like an Auguste Rodin sculpture.

When a tramp with a raggedy jacket, mumbling incoherently, shuffled along Central Park West toward him, stretching out his grimy palm for money, the young man put

The Dakota

his hand into his trouser pocket, pulled out a crumpled ten-dollar bill and thrust it into his hand. Tears trickled down the tramp's face and he kissed the young man full on the cheek. "Go' blezz you, thank you," he muttered and shuffled off, crying softly to himself. Jay Hastings, the twenty-eight-year-old doorman at the building, witnessing the incident from the grimy window of his office, felt warmed at the tiny act of human compassion.

The Dakota, as the apartment building was called, had become famous throughout the world in 1968 when Roman Polanski, the Polish film director, had made it the setting for his horrifying interpretation of Ira Levin's novel, *Rosemary's Baby*.

By 1980, the Dakota had become better known as the closely guarded refuge of a host of celebrities, including Rudolph Nureyev and Lauren Bacall, Leonard Bernstein, Rex Reed, and Ruth Ford. By far the most famous people in the building, however, were the gaunt, wary-eyed couple whose faces graced the pudgy young man's album cover— John and Yoko Lennon.

The next afternoon, Monday, December 8, was even balmier, and Jay Hastings smiled to himself when he saw the man with the record under his arm return to his vigil. This time, there were two other people hanging around outside, waiting for a word, an autograph, a photograph.

Inside the Lennons' apartment, Annie Liebovitz, New York's most respected rock photographer, was in the midst of an extraordinary session. She had been commissioned to photograph the couple for the next issue of *Rolling Stone* magazine. All about the apartment there hung young Sean's paintings, many expensively and beautifully framed. The apartment almost seemed, to a casual visitor, to be a declaration of love between John, the silky-haired Yoko, and their son. Annie had been taken aback by the Lennons' enthusiasm and cooperation, which was in vivid contrast to the laconic, uninterested attitude of most of the famous people she was assigned to photograph. When the results of a session five days earlier had proved disappointing, the couple had been keen for her to return for this second time to try for some more exciting photographs.

John had been to the hairdressers that morning especially to have his hair cut into the long, floppy fringe he had worn as a struggling young musician in Liverpool more than twenty years before. He wore, too, the same style of leather jacket, stovepipe trousers, and huge, black leather cowboy boots he had worn in his youth. As Annie set up her white umbrella flash reflector and pumped through roll after roll of color film, he chatted constantly, reminiscing, looking forward with excitement to the future.

He slipped his boots and jacket off for more photographs, moving from room to room with the lean grace of an alley cat. More than anything, he told Annie, he wanted one perfect photograph which would symbolize and state to the world his feelings for Yoko. He finally decided that he and Yoko should lie down together in the morning room: Yoko fully dressed in jeans and a sweater, and John, clinging desperately to her, naked but for the thin gold wedding ring he wore always on the second finger of his left hand.

When he looked at the resulting photographs, his eyes glowed with excitement: the pictures captured his innermost feelings for Yoko.

Outside, the three fans talked. The pudgy young man, who introduced himself as Mark Chapman, told the other two: "I've flown from Hawaii to get his autograph on the album." The others, noticing the emptiness in Chapman's eyes, suspected he was not quite normal, and left him alone.

As dusk stole over Central Park and the first office-workers began their trudge homeward, John Lennon walked down the steps of the Dakota. He still wore the leather jacket, jeans, and cowboy boots he had worn for the photo session, and he was walking hand-in-hand with Yoko. Chapman had seen their photographs so many times that he knew their faces better than those of his own family. But the rock star was somehow taller, more imposing, slightly less pretty than he had expected him to be.

John smiled as one of the waiting fans snapped photographs, and Chapman proffered a copy of the new album toward him with the usual mumbled request for an autograph. He liked to meet the people who bought his records; it

Mark David Chapman and a co-worker in a Ft. Chaffee, Arkansas, resettlement camp for refuge Vietnamese

reminded him of the days when he had been young and his first fans had hung around for him after his band had played shows in seedy clubs in Liverpool or Hamburg. At first, he didn't even look into the face of the man holding the outstretched album. But, as he handed the record back, their eyes momentarily locked and there was something in the man's faintly superior, half-mocking smile that seemed to send a tremor down the singer's back. He was used to the crazies, the kids with a penchant for acid who gravitated toward him, craved his benediction—but there was an air of glittering madness about this one which set him apart. Chapman wanted to talk, but John skittishly hustled Yoko into their waiting limousine and the pair slid silently into the racetrack of honking yellow cabs.

At the Hit Factory recording studio, everyone was jubilant. John and Yoko's new album—his first in five years—had earned a gold record only two weeks after its release, a triumphant David Geffen, the head of his record company informed them. They had come to add the finishing touches to a song Yoko had written called "Walking on Thin Ice." The record was working out so well that they both thought it was destined to become a surefire hit single. The single had a slight punk sound, yet it was eminently danceable. In some ways, it reminded Lennon of the B-52s, a band he much admired.

Jack Douglas, their producer, thought the fans would prefer to hear John singing than Yoko, but the fact that she sang lead on half the tracks of the new album hadn't seemed to hurt sales. And her voice on "Walking on Thin Ice" was so powerhouse strong that he felt sure it couldn't fail.

The three of them talked briefly about the couple's new album—which they hoped would be ready by autumn. They would start work on mixing and improving the eight tracks they had already laid down early the next morning, they decided. It was 10:30 P.M. now and they were all hungry. John planned to stop off at the Stage Deli to pick up a few sandwiches on their way home.

"Good night, Jack," John had called back as he and Yoko entered the elevator. "See you tomorrow morning, bright and early."

Chapman had spent the six hours since getting his autograph calmly reading J. D. Salinger's *The Catcher in the Rye*. Mark Chapman was six years old when the Beatles released their first record, "Love Me Do." He was nine when the Beatles flew into New York to bring joy back to a nation still shocked and grieving from the needless death of her best-loved president. When he was fifteen they had gone their own ways. He had read every word written about John Lennon and felt, like many people, a closeness and an affinity with him. Like John, he had come from a broken home. Like John, he was so near-sighted that he couldn't see without his glasses. Like John, he had staggered through the miasma of drugs and religion. Like John, he had married a Japanese woman.

Chapman was momentarily startled as John and Yoko's limousine slid to a halt in front of the Dakota. He slipped the book into his pocket.

The chauffeur opened the door so the couple could walk the few steps across the pavement to the Dakota's entrance.

"Mr. Lennon," a voice called from the shadows. And John turned to look into those mad, feverishly glittering eyes once again. For a moment, all time stood still.

"I used to worry about death when I was a kid," John had once said. "Now the fear of it means less and less to me. You know, when we were the rage, we all used to use around-the-clock bodyguards because we genuinely feared for our lives. Now that we've been disbanded for so long, it's a great relief that the terror has disappeared from our lives."

Mark Chapman smiled slightly as he dropped into a combat stance, pulling something hard and metallic from his pocket. Still John stared, momentarily confused, into his eyes. . . .

"In our pleas for peace," he had maintained, "I refuse to be a leader and I'll always show my genitals or do some-

thing which prevents me from being Martin Luther King or Gandhi and getting killed. Because that's what happens to leaders. . . ."

He had practiced long for this moment on the firing range in Honolulu. Calmly, systematically, Mark Chapman squeezed the trigger of his snub-nosed Charter Arms .38 revolver five times. There was a sudden flash of flame, and a string of muffled explosions, like somebody else's Fourth of July party, went off in John's chest.

Chapman felt a soldierly pride in a job well done, little more. He let the pistol slip from his hand. It clattered softly onto the pavement.

"Stop, stop. . . ." Yoko screamed hysterically, though she knew already that it was too late. John still clutched a cassette tape of their last recording session in his right hand; he didn't want to lose that. "I'm shot," he mumbled awkwardly to the doorman as he staggered up the stone steps into the entrance lobby of the Dakota.

John dropped his cassette to the ground with a clatter.

"John's been shot! John's been shot!" Yoko screamed.

Jay Hastings hoped that it was all some dreadful joke. But there was John lying on the ground, blood gurgling from his mouth. His open eyes had a look of astonishment, as if he were unable to comprehend what was happening to him.

"Do you know what you just did?" Hastings screamed at Mark Chapman.

"I just shot John Lennon."

Chapman pulled out his copy of *The Catcher in the Rye* and began to read where he had left off. In the book's flyleaf he had written, "THIS IS MY STATEMENT."

At first, police officers James Moran and William Gamble

did not recognize John Lennon, lying, limbs akimbo, on the ground. He was simply another human being who was going to die unless he was rushed immediately to the hospital. Though they heard his bones cracking as they gingerly lifted him into the back seat of their police car, there was no time to wait for an ambulance. With their cruising lights flashing, they sped through the New York streets in a hopeless race with death toward Roosevelt Hospital.

"It's a big, wide, wonderful world out there. And Yoko and I are going to explore it until we die. . . ."

John Lennon was pronounced dead on arrival.

22

PAUL BURIED HIMSELF in his music when he heard the terrible news—just as he had when his mother died, when the Beatles told him they didn't love him any more and when Wings looked like it was breaking up in the wake of the Japanese fiasco. As the world reeled in horror at this most senseless of deaths, Paul first telephoned Yoko, who told him between sobs that John had always felt warmly toward him— despite caustic remarks in a couple of recent magazine interviews. Then he slipped into his car and drove with Linda and their two smallest children to the studio where they had been working on Wings' new album the previous day.

In the studio, he scarcely spoke about the death which at that moment was bringing tears to the eyes of millions who had never met John Lennon.

"There was," recalls Paddy Maloney, a musician who was working with McCartney that morning, "a kind of unspoken sadness among Paul and the Wings lads like the kind when you lose an old soccer mate. It was subtle and there wasn't any crying or moping about. I don't think it had sunk in yet. Get on with the job was the attitude."

In reality, McCartney's mind was in turmoil, for his relationship with John had become exactly like that of a man who has been divorced by a woman whom he once loved with every fiber of his being. Only a few days before the murder,

Paul had read a stinging interview in which John related his message to Paul regarding Paul's visits to the Dakota—namely, call first. "'You know, just give me a ring.' He was upset by that, but I didn't mean it badly. I just meant that I was taking care of a baby all day and some guy shows up at the door. That was the last time I saw him, but I didn't mean it like that."

By the evening of December 9, as radio stations around the world played nonstop Beatle oldies and television geared up its Lennon documentaries, Paul had begun to clarify his feelings: "I have hidden myself in my work today," he said. "But it keeps flashing into my mind. I feel shattered, angry, and very, very sad. It's just ridiculous. He was pretty rude about me sometimes, but I secretly admired him for it and I always managed to stay in touch with him. There was no question that we weren't friends—I really loved the guy."

Growing heated now: "I think that what has happened will in years to come make people realize that John was an international statesman. He often looked a loony to many people. He made enemies, but he was fantastic. He was a warm man who cared a lot and, with the record 'Give Peace a Chance,' he helped stop the Vietnam war—he made a lot of sense."

Then Paul began suddenly to feel vulnerable. He, George, and Ringo all received cranky, anonymous letters, threatening death, within a few days of John's murder. Ordinarily, they would have laughed at such nonsense. But now Paul hired burly security guards to give twenty-four-hour protection to him and his family.

When it all became too intense, Paul and Linda fled to the Caribbean so Paul could record in the studio which the Beatles' producer George Martin had opened on the lush, tropical island of Montserrat. Even there, though, Paul hired armed guards to protect him. And, when two journalists from Associated Press pursued his rented mini-moke, he panicked and deliberately rammed their car before screaming away with Linda and their children in a cloud of tire smoke. ·

A saddened Paul, two days after John's death

Later, when he had been told who they were, he apologized profusely and told them: "There are a lot of crazy people in the world."

In April, 1981, as Paul took his seat at the premiere of his *Rockshow* film at London's Dominion Theatre, a bearded autograph hunter slipped purposefully toward him. For a moment, there was a stillness as Paul stared at the man, with panic flashing in his eyes. Suddenly, two huge security guards were upon the autograph hunter to bundle him, struggling and protesting, away.

Every stranger was now a potential killer. Never again would Paul be able to relax his guard. . . .

Despite it all, he continued to work at the same frenetic pace he always had: better death than a life without making music. Paul's dedication and his talent had, by 1981, earned him vast rewards—estimated at something approaching $600 million—had made him one of the richest men in Britain. He held all the important recording triumphs listed in *The Guinness Book of World Records*. And his name was finally included in *Who's Who*, that curious list of the British Establishment. Certainly, there seems every likelihood that, when society's attitude to marijuana convictions has become more enlightened, Paul's unique contribution to British life and culture will earn him a knighthood.

George heard of John's death in a dawn phone call from his fifty-year-old sister, Louise, in Florida. He reacted by canceling his recording sessions, locking the doors of Friar Park, and issuing a brief statement: "After all we went through together, I had and still have great love and respect for John. To rob someone of life is the ultimate crime."

His true sense of loss became apparent a few days later when he contacted both Paul and Ringo to ask if they would like to contribute to his next album—an offer which was readily accepted by both. One of the songs on the record, a track called "All Those Years Ago," became a tribute to John.

The elegiac song was prompted partly by guilt. For John had been bitterly hurt when George made no mention whatsoever of him in George's vainglorious $350 book *I, Me, Mine*. But, mainly, he was driven by a sincere feeling of grief and by a desire to tell the world just how much he had genuinely cared for John.

George—like Paul—spoke to Yoko on the phone but decided not to travel to New York to attend John's funeral and personally console her. Instead, he stepped up security at Friar Park and became even more wary of the world outside his wrought-iron front gates.

Ringo was the only ex-Beatle who felt the need to be with Yoko, to share with her his own feeling of devastation. He cut short his holiday in the Bahamas to fly with Barbara Bach to New York as soon as he heard about the shooting.

His car was unable to drive into the Dakota's forecourt because of the thousands of shocked fans who blocked the street outside. As Ringo stepped out to walk across the pavement where John had died only hours before, hands began to snatch at him, pulling at his clothing; harsh voices cried for autographs. He was already deeply shocked, now he began to feel afraid: one of these people had killed John. It was like a scene from Polanski's *Repulsion*. By the time he reached the safety of the block, he was badly shaken.

He was even more distressed when an aide gently told him that Yoko would prefer to see him alone. Without Barbara.

"Please tell her," he said gently, "that we both want to see her."

He found Yoko distraught and little Sean bewildered. Gently, he talked with them, then played with Sean on the floor until the little boy was giggling with pleasure. Death is too big a word for a five-year-old to understand.

Ringo's insistence on not being parted from Barbara was symbolic of the growing closeness between the two of them. At last—like John, George, and Paul—he had found a woman

A garland of flowers is placed at the entrance way to the Dakota in tribute to John Lennon by a mourning fan

who could lend focus to his life; someone he needed to spend every second of every day with.

Paul and George had helped out on Ringo's new album, and Ringo's starring role in *Caveman* confirmed his talent as an actor. At forty, his life truly seemed to have begun again. On April 27, 1981, Ringo and Barbara, in a ceremony attended by Paul McCartney and his family and George and Olivia Harrison, were married. At the reception afterwards, for the first time since Eric Clapton's wedding party, the

*Ringo leaves London's
Marylebone Register
Office with his new bride,
Barbara*

Paul, Linda, and family attending Ringo's wedding

three surviving Beatles jammed together, playing several of their best known songs, including "All You Need Is Love." In many ways, the happy occasion only served to emphasize John's absence.

The three ex-Beatles also got together on a song written as a tribute to John by George entitled "All Those Years Ago," with Paul and Linda singing background vocals and Ringo on drums. The song was included on a new album by George called *Somewhere in England* which was released in May of 1981.

Wings, however, was once again in trouble—Denny Laine told friends that he was quitting the group because Paul was no longer interested in touring. The Beatle who had most needed the thrill and energy of a live audience was settling down.

Yoko, meanwhile, worked to overcome the nightmare of John's death by coolly, logically continuing with what needed to be done. She arranged a secret funeral, placed advertisements in all major world newspapers calling for John's death to be a rallying point for more love—not hatred and suicide. She calmly selected a photograph of herself with John for the cover of *Rolling Stone* magazine. And then she released the single John had helped her to finish off on the night he was shot.

The song was called "Walking on Thin Ice" and John had jumped up and down with excitement when they had recorded it.

"This is going to be your first number one," he had told her.

"I had to release it because he wanted so badly for it to come out," she said. "But what good is it to me if it is a hit now? I can't go and tell John and share it with him any more, can I?"

Tears glistened in her eyes. As her fiftieth birthday loomed closer, Yoko at last had the success she always craved, and she had wealth beyond most people's dreams. Yet, without John, it meant almost nothing.

Julian Lennon

Far away, in Wales, John's eighteen-year-old son Julian was shaken to his soul by his father's death. Though John had abandoned him to live with Yoko, Julian had recently become close to his father once again. Julian too wore wire-rimmed spectacles and center-parted hair so that he looked almost exactly as his father had twelve years before. After John's death, he visited Yoko for a time to console her. Ironically, Julian's loss echoed that which John had suffered at seventeen when his mother, Julia, had been senselessly killed just as they were beginning to reestablish their relationship together.

Julian now showed almost as little public emotion as John had then. But, following the example of his father, he had dissipated all his anger and confusion into making music. He formed a band called the Lennon Drops, which included another young man with an uncanny physical resemblance to Paul McCartney. Though Julian insisted on playing drums, it was undoubtedly his voice which dominated the band. Sometimes, people who listened to him were chilled by the closeness of Julian's singing to that of his father.

"I've got a feeling," he confided, "that my dad would have been proud of this band. . . ."

Perhaps a second generation of Beatles is already on its way.

Picture Credits